FEED ME VEGAN
FOR ALL OCCASIONS

Lucy Watson

FEED ME VEGAN

FOR ALL OCCASIONS

Contents

Introduction

When you change to a vegan or plant-based diet, you go through certain stages — or at least I did. Initially, when I switched to veganism, my main concern was to avoid causing harm to animals rather than with the health benefits, although I know that's a reason many people turn to a vegan diet. I really wanted to find cruelty-free alternatives for all my favourite non-vegan foods.

When I wrote my first *Feed Me Vegan* book I wanted the food to be comforting and similar to what I'd been eating before, and to make the recipes accessible to as many people as possible. I love the recipes in that book — they are a great entry point to a vegan lifestyle. But through this journey I have learnt how to appreciate food so much more — the importance of flavour and the different health benefits plants can give you. The nutrients in plant-based recipes are far superior to non-vegan meals and I appreciate the food I eat for all the benefits it gives me — for my health and for the variety it offers in taste and texture. I have become more aware of what I am putting into my body and like to have a balance in everything I'm cooking and eating now.

The other big thing I wanted to tackle when I wrote this book was the many different scenarios in which veganism can be more difficult. From being in a rush, to preparing something delicious for friends or family, there are so many situations that arise in our busy lives and I want you all to have a handy vegan option for all of them.

At this moment, I'm three years into veganism and I can honestly say it's the best decision I ever made. I appreciate the journey that has brought me to where I am today and love the fact that I am still learning more about food and nutrition every day. I can't wait to continue learning, experiencing new flavours and foods and living a cruelty-free, healthy and happy life. I won't be turning back.

Now go and get stuck into these new recipes. Just make sure those taste buds of yours are prepared for what awaits.

Lucy x

STORE *Cupboard*

Ideally, every kitchen cupboard should be stocked with a range of herbs and spices to add flavour to your cooking, but to take your vegan recipes to the next level, having a great store cupboard will really make all the difference. Since making the switch to veganism a few years ago I've seen my cupboards rapidly expand! You may even find yourself experimenting with new flavour combinations of your own . . . When it comes to herbs and spices, these are the ones you'll see cropping up throughout the book and that I consider essential:

Allspice	**Chinese five-spice powder**	**Garlic granules**	**Rose harissa paste**
Bay leaves	**Cinnamon**	**Ginger**	**Rosemary**
Black onion seeds	**Cumin**	**Mustard seeds**	**Sage**
Caraway seeds	**Curry powder**	**Nutmeg**	**Sea salt**
Cardamom pods	**Fennel seeds**	**Oregano**	**Smoked paprika**
Chilli powder	**Garam masala**	**Paprika**	**Star anise**
			Turmeric

I'd also suggest having a stock of seeds and nuts that you can use to add the finishing touch to recipes, or even just snack on when you're feeling like you need an energy burst. As well as these, there are a few other key ingredients I'd recommend keeping close to hand as they can be great for using in a variety of different recipes:

Acai powder

Agave syrup

Cacao nibs

Chia seeds

Chipotle paste

Egg replacer – a vegan baking essential

Hickory liquid smoke – full of smoky BBQ flavour

Maple syrup

Matcha powder – so great for smoothies!

Miso paste – both white and brown are useful

Nutritional yeast – brings cheesy flavour and depth to recipes

Oils – stock up! Olive, of course, but also coconut, groundnut, sesame and sunflower are worth having

Soy sauce

Tahini

Vanilla paste

Vinegars – cider, rice, white and red wine vinegars are all useful

Wasabi

Since going vegan I've also become so much more aware of single use plastics and how they affect the environment. Although I'm definitely not perfect in terms of how much plastic I use, I do try to avoid it where possible. One great way to do this is to use jar containers for your dried goods. Not only is the organisation extremely satisfying, you can buy ingredients in bulk, which reduces unnecessary plastic packaging.

Feed Me
ON THE GO

Matcha has become a very popular ingredient in recent years, and that's no surprise given its health benefits: it contains antioxidants, fibre and vitamins, and is a great metabolism booster.
As well as that, bananas are brilliant in smoothies; my tip would be to freeze them when they're going a bit brown as it makes the texture of the smoothie so much frothier when you come to blending. This is perfect if you're in a rush or want a quick breakfast.

Matcha SMOOTHIE

SERVES 1 | 2 MINS

80g or about 1 small banana,
   cut into chunks and frozen
1 tsp matcha powder
1 tsp vanilla paste
1–2 drops cardamom extract,
   to taste, or a pinch of ground
   cardamom (optional)
250ml coconut milk
1 tbsp maple syrup (optional)

Put the banana into a food processor or blender and add the remaining ingredients. Blend until smooth, then pour into a glass and enjoy.

As someone who likes the taste of coffee but not the effect it has on my body, I am always open to trying warm drink alternatives. I love the spiciness of chai and it's great for improving digestion and fighting inflammation. The combination of spices in this homemade recipe is great, especially as the ones you get in coffee shops tend to include unnecessary sugars.

Chai LATTE

SERVES 2 | 10 MINS

8 cardamom pods, cracked
10 peppercorns
1 cinnamon stick
2 star anise
1 bay leaf
5cm piece of fresh root ginger,
  peeled and cut into slices
250ml almond milk, preferably
  barista-blend
2 black tea bags
2 tbsp date syrup, agave
  or maple syrup

*Note: You can use agave
or maple syrup in the latte,
but I like the caramel flavours
of date syrup best.*

Put the cardamom pods in a small dry saucepan and add the peppercorns, cinnamon stick and star anise. Heat over a medium heat until fragrant.

Add the remaining ingredients, except the date syrup, and gently heat until hot and infused. Stir in the date syrup, strain into cups and enjoy.

If you like to start the day with something a little more filling, this bircher is perfect! It's super easy to make: prep it the night before so you can grab it in the morning and eat on the way to work/meetings/ the gym. The creaminess of the oats with the rhubarb is really delicious — once again, homemade is so much tastier than store-bought.

CASHEW BIRCHER *with Roasted Rhubarb* —

SERVES 2 | 2 HRS

120g oats
20g sunflower seeds
350ml cashew nut milk
A squeeze of lemon juice
1 tbsp chia seeds
2 tbsp maple syrup

For the roasted rhubarb:
200g rhubarb,
  cut into 4cm lengths
Zest and juice of ½ orange
2 tbsp maple syrup

To serve:
A handful of toasted
  coconut flakes
A handful of chopped
  toasted hazelnuts

Put the oats and the remaining ingredients in a bowl and leave to soak for at least 2 hours, preferably overnight.

Preheat the oven to 180°C (160°C fan, gas 4). Put the rhubarb on a baking tray, squeeze over the orange juice, drizzle with the maple syrup and sprinkle with the orange zest. Bake for 15–20 minutes until the rhubarb is tender and just starting to collapse.

Spoon the oat mixture into two bowls and top with the rhubarb, coconut flakes and hazelnuts to serve.

I felt sandwich fillings were a bit of a let-down when I first went vegan, and although it's getting easier to buy options in some stores, there's still a very limited selection. When I was eighteen I worked as an estate agent and I used to eat egg mayo sandwiches every single day — quite unhealthy to think about it now! But I do miss a good egg sandwich, so I have been working on recreating the textures and flavours. I find tofu, especially silken tofu, the most similar. You can refrigerate a big batch of this filling and use it again: perfect for a work lunch, kids' packed lunch, or if you're just in the mood for a yummy sandwich!

VEGAN *Egg Mayonnaise* TOAST TOPPER

SERVES 2 | 10 MINS

2 tbsp vegan egg replacer, I
   use Follow Your Heart brand
1 tsp vegan butter
50g vegan mayonnaise
½ tsp Dijon mustard
Zest of ½ lemon, plus a
   squeeze of lemon juice
90g silken tofu
Sea salt and freshly ground
   black pepper
Toasted rye bread and
   watercress, to serve

*Note: The brand of egg
replacer used makes a huge
difference to the taste so
make sure it's one you like!*

Put the egg replacer in a bowl, add 115ml water and whisk together. Put the butter in a small saucepan over a medium heat. Add the egg replacer mixture and scramble it, using a wooden spoon, for 6–8 minutes until cooked through. Leave to one side to cool completely.

Mix together the mayonnaise, mustard, lemon zest and juice.

Chop the silken tofu and the scrambled egg replacer into small pieces using a knife, then fold this into the mayonnaise mixture. Season to taste with salt and pepper.

Spread the mixture on toasted rye bread and top with a few watercress leaves to serve.

Another former favourite of mine, and who would have thought you could recreate it using chickpeas?! The texture of the mashed chickpeas is very similar to that of fish, and once marinated it tastes delicious. It's a clean, high-protein alternative to tuna — as with the egg mayo, I tend to make a batch as it can also be used in salads, sandwiches or even on baked potatoes with some sweetcorn.

VEGAN *Tuna Mayonnaise*

SERVES 4–6 | 5 MINS

400g tin chickpeas,
  rinsed and drained
Zest and juice of ½ lemon
60g vegan mayonnaise
1 tsp sweet white miso
1 tbsp nutritional yeast
½ red onion, finely chopped
50g sundried tomatoes,
  roughly chopped
Sea salt and freshly ground
  black pepper

Put the chickpeas in a bowl and crush with a fork until you have a have coarse-textured mash. Add the remaining ingredients and season to taste with salt and pepper.

Use to fill sandwiches or jacket potatoes. Store in a sealed container in the fridge for up to 5 days.

A tasty and healthy soup with a kick! Quick and simple to prepare, this is a recipe that makes eating well seem super easy.

Super-Green SOUP

SERVES 4 | 30 MINS

1 tbsp coconut oil
3 shallots, finely sliced
2cm piece of fresh root ginger,
   peeled and grated
1 green jalapeño chilli,
   deseeded and finely chopped
1 fat garlic clove, minced
1 head of broccoli, stalk
   peeled and roughly chopped,
   and head broken into
   small florets
600ml vegetable stock
150g frozen peas
400ml coconut cream
120g baby spinach
1 small bunch of mint leaves
Juice of 1–2 limes, to taste
Sea salt and freshly ground
   black pepper

To serve:
Chilli flakes
Coconut cream

Put the coconut oil in a saucepan over a medium heat. Add the shallots, ginger, chilli and garlic with a pinch of salt, and cook until the shallots are soft and translucent.

Add the broccoli to the mix and stir everything together. Add the vegetable stock, peas and coconut cream. Gradually bring to the boil, then lower the heat and simmer for 15–20 minutes until the broccoli is tender.

Add the spinach and mint, then blend until smooth. Season with salt and pepper, and add lime juice to taste. Ladle into bowls and serve.

Garnish with a sprinkle of chilli flakes and a drizzle of coconut cream.

HOW TO MAKE THE PERFECT *Sushi Rice*

SERVES 2–3 | UNDER 15 MINS

250g sushi rice
1 tsp sugar
¼ tsp salt
40ml rice vinegar

Wash the rice in a sieve under cold running water until the water runs clear. Put the rice in a saucepan and add enough water so that the level of the water is about 5mm above the rice. Put the saucepan over a high heat and bring to the boil, stirring from time to time.

As soon as the water is boiling, reduce the heat to the lowest setting, then cover and leave to cook. Check the rice after 6 minutes by carefully removing a grain of rice without disturbing the remaining grains. It should be tender with a bite in the centre. If the rice is cooked, remove the pan from the heat. If the rice is still too firm, leave the pan on the heat but make sure it isn't too dry or it will burn the base of the pan — add a splash of hot water to finish the rice, if needed.

Using a wooden spoon, take out the rice from the pan and transfer it to a bowl — don't be tempted to scrape away any rice that is stuck to the base of the pan, because this will be damaged and won't taste good.

In a small bowl, stir the sugar and salt into the rice vinegar, then keep stirring until the sugar has dissolved. Stir this mixture into the rice, then leave to cool down a little before using.

Your rice is now ready to use for onigiri (opposite) or sushi (page 132).

Not a recipe for the lazy chef, but totally worth it. The juicy centre is delicious and these are really fun to make — so worth it if you're looking for a recipe to impress your friends or if you're in a creative mood!

ONIGIRI *filled with Mushroom & Kale*

SERVES 2 | 45 MINS

1 quantity of perfect sushi rice
  (see opposite), kept warm

For the filling:
2 tsp vegan butter
120g oyster mushrooms,
  torn into small pieces
1 garlic clove, crushed
30g kale, ribs removed
  and shredded
100ml soya cream
1 tsp brown miso

To serve:
1 sheet of nori seaweed
Togarashi
Pickled ginger
Wasabi
Soy sauce

To prepare the onigiri filling, put 1 tsp of the butter in a saucepan over a medium heat and add the mushrooms. Cook until tinged golden brown around the edges, then remove from the pan and keep to one side. Add the garlic and kale to the pan with the remaining butter, and cook until the garlic is fragrant and the kale is wilted. Return the mushrooms to the pan and add the cream and miso. Cook for 2 minutes to reduce slightly.

If you are right-handed, wet your left hand and scoop up a portion of your prepared sushi rice. Flatten the rice with your right hand to cover the palm of your left hand.

Spoon a little of the filling into the centre of the rice and, using your hand, fold the rice over the filling, compacting the rice into a ball. Sometimes you may need to add a little extra rice at the end to completely encase the filling. Keep wetting your hands to prevent the rice from sticking. You can leave the onigiri shaped as balls or you can mould them into a triangular shape.

Garnish the onigiri with nori seaweed, togarashi and pickled ginger. Serve with wasabi and soy sauce on the side.

*O*ver the last year I have finally learned to really appreciate salads. I used to be so anti-salad and barely ever ate any leaves or veggies! What makes this Caesar is the coconut bacon — it gives it a hint of sweetness and a delicious crunch along with the hazelnuts.

Coconut Bacon & Hazelnut CAESAR SALAD

SERVES 2 | UNDER 30 MINS

For the coconut bacon:
2 tsp maple syrup
2 tsp soy sauce
2 drops of hickory liquid smoke
½ tsp smoked paprika
50g toasted coconut flakes

For the salad:
50g blanched hazelnuts,
  roughly chopped
80g wholemeal ciabatta
  bread, torn into
  medium-sized pieces
1 tbsp extra virgin olive oil
4 baby gem lettuces or 1
  cos lettuce, separated into
  individual leaves and cut
4 tbsp grated vegan
  Parmesan cheese
Sea salt and freshly ground
  black pepper

For the dressing:
½ garlic clove
2 tbsp vegan mayonnaise
Zest and juice of ½ lemon
1 small red onion, finely sliced
1 tsp Dijon mustard

Preheat the oven to 180˚C (160˚C fan, gas 4) and line a baking tray with baking parchment. To make the coconut bacon, in a medium bowl mix together the maple syrup, soy sauce, hickory liquid smoke and paprika. Throw in the coconut flakes and toss to coat evenly in the mixture. Spread out in a single layer on the prepared baking tray and toast in the oven for 10 minutes, tossing them after 5 minutes to ensure an even cook.

Put the hazelnuts on another baking tray and toast in the oven for 10 minutes or until golden brown and fragrant.

Put the wholemeal bread in a mixing bowl and add the oil, then season with salt and pepper, and toss to coat. Put on a baking tray and toast in the oven for 15 minutes or until golden brown and evenly toasted.

Meanwhile, make the dressing. Pound the garlic with a good pinch of salt using a mortar and pestle. Stir in the mayonnaise, mustard, lemon zest and juice, loosening with a splash of water if needed. Mix in the onion and stir through the dressing, then leave to macerate for 5 minutes.

Toss the salad leaves in the dressing, then throw in the croutons, the coconut bacon and the toasted hazelnuts. Sprinkle with the Parmesan cheese and serve.

*L*ike a pot noodle but a million times healthier! I love how this recipe looks in jars, and it's so easy for meal prepping: when you're ready to eat you just pour hot water and stir. Quick and easy, perfect for when you're on the go and something to impress your colleagues!

Healthy NOODLE JAR

SERVES 1 | 10 MINS

1 nest of fine egg noodles

90g edamame beans

2 spring onions, finely sliced

3 radishes, finely sliced

1 carrot, spiralised or grated

A handful of shredded greens

50g silken tofu, cut into
    small dice

1 tbsp brown miso paste

1cm piece of fresh root ginger,
    peeled and grated

Chilli sauce and a wedge
    of lime, to serve

Cook the noodles in a saucepan of boiling water for 3–4 minutes until tender or according to the packet instructions. Cook the edamame beans in a saucepan of boiling water for 3 minutes, then drain and refresh under cold water — or thaw if you're using frozen beans. Layer the noodles, vegetables, tofu and flavourings in a medium-sized lidded jar, finishing with the miso and grated ginger.

When ready to eat, pour over enough hot water to cover everything, then give it a good stir. Serve with chilli sauce and a wedge of lime to squeeze over the top.

This has to be one of my favourite quick lunches. The flavours go so well together: the mustard gives everything a really nice kick, especially when combined with the maple for that touch of sweetness. I use Violife's ready-sliced cheese, but you can use whichever you prefer. The ready-sliced is perfect for toasties though . . .

Grilled Cheese & Sauerkraut
TOASTED SANDWICH

SERVES 1 | 10 MINS

2 tsp Dijon mustard

1 tsp fresh dill

½ tsp maple syrup

2 slices of good-quality
   crusty bread

50g vegan Cheddar cheese,
   grated

70g beetroot and red cabbage
   sauerkraut (page 50)

2 tsp vegan butter

In a bowl, mix the mustard with the dill and maple syrup, then spread this mixture on one side of each piece of bread. Layer the cheese and sauerkraut onto one slice, then put the remaining slice of bread on top and squash down firmly.

Heat the butter in a frying pan over a medium heat, add the sandwich and cook on both sides until it's golden brown and the cheese is melted. Serve.

HOW TO MAKE *Nut Butter*

MAKES 1 JAR | 40 MINS

250g mixed nuts (such as
   macadamia nuts, cashew
   nuts, Brazil nuts and
   pistachio nuts)
A pinch of salt

Optional extras:
1 tbsp melted coconut oil
1 tsp ground cinnamon
1 tbsp maple syrup
1–2 tbsp cocoa powder

Preheat the oven to 180°C (160°C fan, gas 4). Put the
nuts in a single layer on a baking tray and roast for
15–20 minutes until toasted, golden brown and fragrant.

Leave the nuts to cool for 15 minutes, then tip into a
food processor and blitz until you have a smooth butter.
Add the salt.

If you feel like being experimental, add coconut oil and
cinnamon or maple syrup for added sweetness, or you
can easily create a Nutella vibe by simply adding some
cocoa powder.

Since going vegan I have become much more aware of nutritional value and find that many so-called 'healthy' bars you can buy have a huge amount of added sugar and aren't actually all that healthy for you! Make up a batch of these and you'll find it so much easier to avoid the temptation of sugar-filled snacking.

Hazelnut, Oat & Cranberry SEED BARS

MAKES 14 BARS

| UNDER 40 MINS

160g oats

5 tbsp desiccated coconut

50g hazelnuts, roughly
   chopped

3 tbsp ground flaxseed

45g sunflower seeds

30g pumpkin seeds

3 tbsp dried cranberries

4 tbsp nut butter (see opposite
   for nut butter recipe)

4 tbsp coconut oil

100ml brown rice syrup

A pinch of salt

Preheat the oven to 180°C (160°C fan, gas 4). Grease and line a shallow 18 × 24cm baking tin with baking parchment. Put the oats in a mixing bowl and add the coconut, hazelnuts, seeds and cranberries, then stir to combine.

Put the nut butter (I used store-bought hazelnut butter) in a small saucepan and add the coconut oil, rice syrup and salt. Heat, stirring, over a low heat until melted and combined. Mix the wet ingredients into the dry ingredients until fully combined and coated.

Tip this mixture onto the prepared baking tray and smooth out into an even, compacted layer using the back of a spoon. Bake for 20–25 minutes until tinged golden brown around the edges and fragrant. Leave to cool completely before cutting into fingers.

Acai (pronounced 'ah-sah-ee') has become very popular over the last few years and I can understand why! The acai berry has so many health benefits and is bursting with antioxidants. Though actual acai berries are very hard to source, using acai powder means you can still get all the benefits. This is a perfect recipe for on a warm day as it's super-refreshing, especially with some coconut flakes sprinkled on top.

Acai BOWL

SERVES 1 | 2 MINS

60g banana, cut into
   chunks and frozen
1–2 tsp acai powder, to taste
90g frozen berries
200ml coconut milk from
   a carton (not a tin)
1 tsp vanilla bean paste

For the topping:
A handful of frozen
   blackberries
1 tbsp chia seeds
1 tbsp toasted coconut flakes
A handful of mint leaves

Put the banana and the remaining ingredients into a blender and blend until smooth. Pour into a bowl and top with the frozen berries, chia seeds, toasted coconut flakes and mint. Sprinkle with a few red currants or toasted pumpkin seeds, and serve.

This recipe needs a bit of time chilling, so I try to prep everything the night before, or get up a bit earlier in the morning when I know I want to make it. It's so worth it though: not only are chia seeds yummy but they have many health benefits including antioxidants, omega 3 fats, vitamins and minerals. This is a sweet dish — great for dessert or a decadent breakfast!

COCONUT & MANGO CHIA PUDDING
with Cardamom & Lime

SERVES 4 | 30 MINS

Seeds from 2 cardamom pods
400ml can coconut milk
100g chia seeds
1 tsp vanilla bean paste
2 tbsp maple syrup
Zest of ½ lime, plus a
    squeeze of lime juice,
    to taste
1 large ripe mango, peeled
    and sliced
1 lime, to serve

Grind the cardamom seeds in a mortar and pestle to a fine powder. Pour the coconut milk into a bowl and stir in the chia seeds. Add the vanilla, ground cardamom, maple syrup and lime zest. Squeeze in a little lime juice to balance the acidity, then leave to one side for the mixture to gel for 20–30 minutes.

Spoon into bowls and top with sliced mango. Zest the remaining lime and sprinkle the zest over the mango, then cut the lime into wedges and serve to squeeze over.

Feed Me

HEALTHY

I first started drinking these lattes when I fell ill one freezing winter and couldn't seem to shift my cold. I've always been prone to colds, though I don't get them nearly as much since making the switch in my diet. However, though these started off as a way of trying to drink turmeric as I know it has a lot of medicinal health benefits, I actually choose to drink them instead of a coffee now! This recipe has the right amount of sweetness for me but you can always reduce the amount of maple syrup if you wish.

Turmeric LATTE

SERVES 2 | 10 MINS

5cm fresh turmeric, peeled
  and cut into small chunks,
  or 1 tsp ground turmeric
400ml almond milk
  (I prefer barista-blend)
1 tsp ground ginger
½ tsp ground cinnamon
1 tbsp white almond butter
1 tbsp maple syrup

Put the turmeric in a small saucepan and add the milk, ginger and cinnamon, then bring to the boil slowly using the lowest heat setting. Put the hot milk mixture into a food processor or blender, add the nut butter and maple syrup, and blend until the milk is foamy and vibrant golden in colour. Pour into two mugs and serve.

Super-Green JUICE

Brilliant if you've had a few too many takeaways or a big weekend and need a detox — filled with nutrients and superfoods! A lot of green juices can taste a bit earthy but this one has the perfect balance of sweet and savoury flavours.

SERVES 2 | 2 MINS

1 lime, peel and pith cut off
2 green apples
90g spinach
250g fennel

A handful of Brussels sprouts
A small bunch of mint
Ice cubes, to serve

Push all the ingredients, except the ice cubes, through a juicer. Pour over the ice cubes into two glasses and serve.

Ginger, Carrot & Orange JUICE

This juice is a serious immune booster and the kind of thing I make if I'm really under the weather or feeling run down. I also love to have one post-workout as it's really refreshing but not too filling — just what you want when that post-gym hunger descends!

SERVES 2 | 2 MINS

3 oranges, peel and pith removed
4 large carrots
A thumb-sized piece of fresh root ginger, or to taste
A thumb-sized piece of fresh turmeric, or to taste
Ice, to serve

Note: Apart from the oranges, don't bother removing the peel from the remaining ingredients. Just make sure you give them a quick wash beforehand. Most of the nutrients can be found in the peels, so it's best to leave them on.

Push all the ingredients, except the ice, through a juicer. Pour over the ice cubes into two glasses and enjoy!

Beetroot is an all-round wonder vegetable with many health benefits including vitamin C, potassium and vitamin B folate. It's great in smoothies, salads, dips and even roasted, so if you're feeling like a nutritious pick-me-up then this is the one for you!

Beetroot, Ginger & Hibiscus Tea
SMOOTHIE

SERVES 2 | 2 MINS

100g frozen berries
1 piece of stem ginger
  from a jar
1 cooked beetroot (without
  vinegar), roughly chopped
200ml brewed hibiscus tea,
  chilled

Put all the ingredients into a blender and process until smooth. Pour into two glasses and serve.

I have recently become obsessed with sauerkraut; I absolutely LOVE it on top of a vegan burger — with some vegan cheese, of course. Not only is it delicious but it's also a great source of vitamins and other vital minerals — who knew fermented foods could be so good for you?! Once you've made up a batch you can keep it in the fridge for adding to any meals you fancy, and it's also amazing for toasties (see page 35).

Beetroot & Red Cabbage SAUERKRAUT

MAKES 1 LARGE JAR | PREP 1½ HRS PLUS 1–6 WEEKS FERMENTING

1 small red cabbage
1 small beetroot,
  coarsely grated
1 tbsp sea salt
1 tbsp caraway seeds

Carefully remove 2 of the outer leaves from the cabbage and keep to one side. Use a mandolin, a food processor or a large, sharp knife to finely shred the remaining cabbage.

Mix the shredded cabbage and beetroot well in a large mixing bowl with the salt to distribute the salt evenly throughout the cabbage. Leave to sweat and go limp for 1 hour.

By now you should be able to see that the cabbage has released some water. You might want to wear rubber gloves for the next stage, to prevent your hands from staining. Using your hands, squeeze and massage the cabbage using some force to reduce the volume of the cabbage and release as much of the water as possible, reserving the brine in case you need it later. Continue doing this for 5 minutes. Mix in the caraway.

Pack the cabbage tightly into a large open-necked jar (ideally the opening of the jar will be wide enough to fit in a clenched fist), using your fist or the end of a rolling pin to pack it down. When all the cabbage is packed into the jar, you should have enough cabbage brine to cover the top of the shredded cabbage by about 2cm. If necessary, you can use some of the brine that is left in the bowl to top this level up. Make sure that all the cabbage is submerged below the level of the brine; you don't want to leave any straggly bits. *Continued overleaf.*

Fold 1 or 2 of the large outer leaves you removed earlier and pack them into the top of the jar to help keep the shredded cabbage submerged under the brine.

Put the lid on the jar loosely and leave the jar somewhere dark at room temperature for at least 5 days. The length of time before the sauerkraut will be ready will vary, but it will usually be a little quicker in the warmer months. After 5 days, carefully remove the top cabbage leaf and taste a little of the sauerkraut to see if it is ready — it should have a sour taste. You can leave the sauerkraut to ferment from anywhere between 2 and 6 weeks depending on how sour you like it. Once fermented, it will keep for months in the fridge.

QUICK PICKLE: Bay & Black Pepper Preserved Lemons

MAKES 1 JAR | PREP 20–30 MINS PLUS 2–3 DAYS CURING

4 bay leaves
60g sea salt flakes
2 tbsp sugar
3 unwaxed lemons
1 tsp black peppercorns, lightly crushed

Put the bay leaves in a spice grinder or bullet blender and add the salt and sugar.

Slice the lemons thinly, removing any pips as you go. Layer the lemon slices in a sterilised, medium-sized jar, sprinkling some of the salt mixture and peppercorns between each layer and pressing them down. Continue until all the lemon slices have been used and they are packed into the jar as tightly as possible. Seal the jar.

The lemons can be used after 2–3 days, but I find that they are just perfect after a week. Store in a cool dry place for up to 6 weeks. You can find recipes that include preserved lemons on pages 52, 66 and 116.

These are a classic go-to evening supper — for many people, and for good reason. Before I went vegan I used to dress my peppers with lashings of dairy cheese, but I have to say this take is much yummier (and you can still add vegan cheese if you wish). They do take a while to prepare but are great to make in batches so you have leftovers and lunches.

Stuffed PEPPERS

SERVES 4

| **ABOUT 1½ HOURS**

8 red peppers

2 tbsp olive oil, plus extra
  for greasing

60g pine nuts

2 small onions, finely chopped

2 garlic cloves, crushed

450g frozen vegan mince

3 tsp ground allspice

1 tsp chilli powder

2 tsp paprika

1 tsp ground cinnamon

2 tsp ground cumin

450g tomatoes, roughly
  chopped

100g preserved lemons,
  finely chopped

110g basmati rice

80g tomato purée

3 tbsp sundried tomato paste

8 bay leaves

Sea salt and freshly ground
  black pepper

Dressed green salad, to serve

Preheat the oven to 180°C (160°C fan, gas 4). Cut off the tops of the peppers and keep to one side. Scoop out and discard the white membranes and seeds. Rub inside and out of the peppers with a little oil, and season generously with salt and pepper. Stand the peppers upright in a flameproof casserole, packing them in tightly.

Put the pine nuts in a dry pan and toast over a medium-high heat, tossing regularly, for 1–2 minutes, or until golden brown. Leave to one side.

Put the oil in a non-stick wok or large saucepan over a medium heat and stir-fry the onions and garlic until soft and translucent. Add the mince and spices, and cook until the mince is defrosted and lightly browned. Add the chopped tomatoes and 200ml water. Bring to the boil, then reduce the heat and simmer for 15 minutes or until the tomatoes start to break down. Stir in the pine nuts, preserved lemons and rice. Season to taste with salt and pepper.

Fill the peppers with the mince mixture. Put the tomato purée and sun-dried tomato paste in a jug and stir in 400ml hot water. Pour a little of the liquid into each of the peppers, add the reserved pepper tops and pour the remaining liquid into the casserole. Slide the bay leaves in among the peppers.

Put the casserole on the hob and bring to the boil, then cover and transfer to the oven. Cook for 35 minutes, then remove the lid and cook for a further 20–25 minutes until the peppers start to brown and the sauce in the base is reduced a little.

To serve the peppers, spoon over a little of the sauce from the base of the casserole and serve with a dressed green salad.

I would never normally think to include mango in a salad but all these ingredients go so well together! I first tasted a similar recipe on Hamilton Island in Australia, and I knew I had to recreate it when I got home. It's refreshing and delicious with the ideal mix of sweet and savoury!

Avocado, Mango & Pomegranate SALAD —

SERVES 2 | 15 MINS

1 ripe mango, peeled and
   cut into small cubes
250g pouch ready-to-eat
   mixed grains (I used a red
   and white quinoa mix, but
   any grain mixes will work)
30g pumpkin seeds
1 avocado, peeled and
   cut into cubes
A small bunch of mint,
   leaves finely chopped
A small bunch of coriander,
   leaves finely chopped
   (optional)
Seeds from ½ pomegranate
Sea salt and freshly ground
   black pepper

For the dressing:
3 tbsp mild virgin olive oil
1 tbsp cider vinegar
Zest and juice of 1 lime

Put half the mango in a blender and add the dressing ingredients. Season with salt and pepper, then process until smooth, adding a splash of water if needed to create a pourable consistency.

Warm through the grains according to the packet instructions. Toast the pumpkin seeds in a dry frying pan until they start to pop and crack.

Put the remaining cubed mango and the avocado in a large serving bowl or on a platter and add the grains, then fold through the chopped herbs and pumpkin seeds. Add half the dressing and pomegranate seeds and toss to mix. Sprinkle over the remaining pomegranate and drizzle with the remaining dressing to serve.

Tempeh is one of those foods that can take some getting used to. If I'm honest, I didn't like it when I first began eating it, but the more I tried it, the more I began to like it. Tempeh is given flavour by what you marinate it in, on its own it can be a bit 'meh'. This salad is super healthy but packed with nutritional value and flavour — perfect if you're in the mood for something a bit lighter, but still want 'gains', as my boyfriend would call it.

TEMPEH SALAD *with*
Toasted Coconut & Avocado

SERVES 4 | 20 MINS

230g tempeh, cut into
  2.5cm cubes
200g green beans
1 small cucumber, cut into
  ribbons with a vegetable
  peeler, seeds discarded
1 avocado, pitted, peeled
  and cut into cubes
160g mangetout,
  cut in half lengthways
80g toasted coconut flakes
1 tbsp black sesame seeds
Leaves from a small bunch
  of mint
1 red chilli, deseeded
  and finely sliced

For the dressing:
2cm piece of fresh root
  ginger, peeled and grated
2 garlic cloves, crushed
Juice of 1 lime
2 heaped tbsp tahini
1 tbsp agave nectar
1 tbsp sesame oil
2 tbsp groundnut oil
2 tsp white miso
Sea salt and freshly ground
  black pepper

For the tempeh marinade:
4 tsp white miso
3 tsp soy sauce
1 tbsp maple syrup
½ tsp chilli powder
A squeeze of lime juice

To make the dressing, put the dressing ingredients in a bowl and add a splash of water. Whisk together and season to taste.

To make the tempeh marinade, put the ingredients in a bowl and whisk them together. Thread the tempeh onto four skewers and brush them with the marinade. Cook the skewers on a hot griddle over a high heat for 6–8 minutes until golden and charred on all sides.

Put the green beans into a pan of boiling water and cook for 2 minutes to blanch them, then drain in a colander and refresh under cold water.

Arrange the beans and the remaining salad ingredients on a large platter, sprinkling the black sesame seeds and drizzling over the dressing. Lay the skewers on top and serve.

How pretty?! Not only that, but this salad is super yummy! The tofu helps make it filling, and all in all it's gorgeous for a summer lunch. I'd leave out the coriander if making it for myself but I know that some people are real fans so wanted to make sure the option is there. We all have days where we're in the mood for something a bit lighter and this is ideal.

POMELO SALAD *with* Sesame-Crusted Tofu

SERVES 6 | 45 MINS

1 pomelo
1 pink grapefruit
1 navel or blood orange
80g cashew nuts
100g radishes, thinly sliced
1 radicchio lettuce,
  roughly sliced
A small bunch of mint,
  leaves chopped
A small bunch of coriander,
  leaves and stems finely
  chopped
1 red chilli, deseeded
  and finely chopped

For the dressing:
Juice of 1½ limes
30g palm sugar, grated
1 shallot, finely chopped
40ml rice vinegar
60ml sesame oil

For the fried tofu:
40g sesame seeds
2 tbsp cornflour
280g block firm tofu,
  cut into thick slices
Sea salt and freshly
  ground black pepper
Groundnut oil, for
  shallow-frying

Using a sharp knife, cut a thin slice of peel and pith from each end of the pomelo. Put cut-side down on a board and cut off the peel and pith in strips. Remove any remaining pith. Cut out each segment leaving the membrane behind. Repeat with the grapefruit and orange. Or, alternatively, you can slice the peeled orange into attractive rounds.

Put the cashew nuts in a dry frying pan and toast over a medium-high heat until golden, tossing them regularly. Leave to one side.

Arrange the citrus fruits, radishes, lettuce, herbs and chilli on a large serving platter.

To make the dressing, put the lime juice and palm sugar in a small bowl and whisk until dissolved. Whisk in the remaining dressing ingredients.

To make the fried tofu, mix together the sesame seeds and cornflour, then season generously with salt and pepper and put on a plate. Coat the tofu slices in the sesame seed mixture, pressing each side of the tofu into the coating. Heat some of the oil in a non-stick frying pan and fry the tofu until golden brown on each side.

Top the salad with the fried tofu and toasted cashew nuts. Spoon the dressing over the salad to serve.

This soup is packed with both protein and flavour. You can have it on its own or with tortilla chips as more of a sharing dip. I don't know many people who wouldn't enjoy this — it's such a comforting recipe.

Chipotle Black Bean & Quinoa Soup
WITH CORN

SERVES 2 | UNDER 30 MINS

1 onion, finely chopped

1 tbsp groundnut oil or other
  similar flavourless oil,
  plus extra for brushing

1 carrot, diced

2 garlic cloves, crushed

2 tbsp tomato purée

1 heaped tsp chipotle paste

400g tin black beans,
  rinsed and drained

1 bay leaf

25g quinoa, rinsed
  and drained

700ml vegetable stock

Juice of 1 lime

1 corn on the cob

1 tsp red chilli, finely sliced

A handful of coriander leaves

½ avocado, diced

A handful of tortilla chips
  and 2 lime wedges, to serve

Sea salt and freshly ground
  black pepper

Put the onion and oil in a saucepan and add the carrot and garlic. Cook over a medium heat until the onion is soft and translucent. Add the tomato purée and chipotle, and continue cooking for 1 minute.

Add the black beans, bay leaf, quinoa and stock. Bring to the boil, then reduce the heat and simmer gently for 15–20 minutes until the quinoa has cooked and the soup has thickened slightly. Stir in the lime juice, and season to taste with salt and pepper.

Lightly oil the corn and season it generously. Heat a griddle pan over a high heat and char the corn on all sides. Strip the kernels from the cob using a sharp knife.

Ladle the soup into two bowls and top with the charred corn, sliced chilli, coriander leaves and avocado. Serve with tortilla chips and a wedge of lime on the side.

This soup is similar to a gazpacho, but with lighter flavours and a refreshing feel to it. Ideal for a light summer lunch, or you could have it as a starter for a dinner party — I'm picturing a summer evening in the garden, as this looks so cute.

Chilled Cucumber, Mint & Almond SOUP

SERVES 4 | UNDER 10 MINS

2 cucumbers, peeled
  and roughly chopped
400g plain soya yogurt
1 garlic clove, peeled
  and left whole
A few leaves of tarragon
A few leaves of mint
2 tbsp white wine vinegar
2 tbsp extra virgin olive oil
50g stale white bread
A squeeze of lemon juice
Sea salt and freshly ground
  black pepper

To garnish:
Toasted flaked almonds
Mint leaves
Croutons
A drizzle of extra virgin
  olive oil

Put all the ingredients, except the lemon juice, into a food processor or blender and process until smooth. Season to taste with salt, pepper and a squeeze of lemon juice. Pour into four bowls, top with some toasted flaked almonds, mint leaves and croutons and drizzle over some extra virgin olive oil.

I love anything with homemade hummus, but especially tonnes of delicious veggies! Packed with flavour and texture, this bowl does not disappoint. It's easy to make and sure to fill you up — and completely guilt-free!

MOROCCAN COUSCOUS BOWL *with Roasted Root Vegetables, Hummus & Crispy Chickpeas*

SERVES 2 | UNDER 45 MINS

120g parsnips, cut into
  even-sized chunks
300g heritage carrots,
  cut into even-sized chunks
1½ tbsp oil
1 tsp garlic granules
1 tsp cumin seeds
1 tsp ground cumin
Sea salt and freshly ground
  black pepper
2 preserved lemon slices,
  to serve (page 51)

For the couscous:
160g couscous
2 tbsp extra virgin olive oil
A handful of mint, leaves
  roughly chopped
A handful of coriander, leaves
  roughly chopped and stems
  finely chopped
4 pitted Medjool dates,
  roughly chopped
4 tbsp pomegranate seeds
A handful of baby spinach,
  finely chopped
1 tbsp lemon juice

For the crispy chickpeas:
200g tinned chickpeas,
  rinsed, drained and patted
  dry with kitchen paper
¼ tsp ground cumin
¼ tsp garlic granules
1 tbsp olive oil
¼ tsp salt

For the hummus:
200g tinned chickpeas,
  rinsed and drained
1 tsp tahini
Juice of ½ lemon
1 tsp extra virgin olive oil

Preheat the oven to 180°C (160°C fan, gas 4). Put the root vegetables in a small roasting tin and toss with the oil, garlic granules and spices. Season with salt and pepper, and roast for 30–35 minutes or until tinged golden brown and cooked through.

Put the couscous in a bowl with 1 tbsp of the oil and stir to coat all the couscous granules. Cover with hot water, then cover immediately with cling film. Leave for 10 minutes to absorb the water. Fluff up with a fork. Stir in the herbs, dates, pomegranate seeds and spinach. Whisk the remaining oil with the lemon juice and stir through the couscous. Season to taste with salt and pepper.

To make the crispy chickpeas, put the chickpeas in a bowl and toss them in the cumin and garlic granules. Heat the oil in a saucepan over a medium heat and add the chickpeas, then cook until crispy. Sprinkle with the salt.

To make the hummus, put all the ingredients into a bullet blender or mini blender and add 2–3 tbsp water. Process until smooth, adding a splash more water if needed. Season to taste.

To serve, spoon the couscous into two bowls and top with the root vegetables, hummus and crispy chickpeas. Serve with 2 preserved lemon slices to finish.

Warming Vegetable & White Bean Stew
WITH MUSTARD DUMPLINGS

Stews are something I never really used to eat, but when you go vegan you want to try a vegan version of everything! Veggie stews scream comfort and warmth but this one is so much more than that, with the meatiness of the vegan chorizo and the soft dumplings to top it off. It takes a bit of time to cook (and if you're short on time I'd suggest swapping in ready-to-cook beans) but once it's in the oven you can pretty much leave it to let all those great flavours come together.

SERVES 4–6 | ABOUT 6 HRS

200g dried white beans

1 tbsp olive oil

2 onions, thinly sliced

3 garlic cloves, crushed

130g vegan chorizo sausages, cut into thick slices

2 tbsp sundried tomato paste

230ml vegan red wine

2 bay leaves

2 thyme sprigs

3 large carrots, cut into thick slices

2 celery sticks, cut into 2cm lengths

2 tbsp balsamic vinegar

400g tin tomatoes

2 tbsp tomato purée

750ml vegetable stock

For the dumplings:

130g plain flour

Zest of 1 lemon

A small bunch of dill, fronds roughly chopped

75g vegetable suet

2 tbsp Dijon mustard

Put the white beans in a saucepan, cover with water and bring to the boil. Boil the beans for 10 minutes, then turn off the heat and leave to soak for 3 hours. Drain the beans after they have soaked. Leave to one side.

Preheat the oven to 150°C (130°C fan, gas 2). Put the oil in a flameproof casserole and cook the onions over a medium heat until soft and translucent. Add the garlic and chorizo, and cook for 2 minutes. Stir in the tomato paste and cook for 1 minute.

Add the wine, bay leaves and thyme, and allow to bubble away for 4–5 minutes until reduced. Add the remaining ingredients, including the soaked beans. Bring everything to the boil, cover and transfer the casserole to the oven and cook for 2½ hours.

Meanwhile, to make the dumplings, sift the flour into a mixing bowl and stir in the lemon zest and chopped dill. Add the suet and rub into the flour with your fingertips. Add the mustard and enough cold water to bring the dough together. Roll into walnut-sized balls.

Add a splash of water to the stew if it's looking a little dry. Put the dumplings on top of the stew, increase the oven temperature to 190°C (170°C fan, gas 5), put the lid back on and cook for a further 30 minutes until the dumplings are fluffy and firm, then serve.

Chilli & Lemongrass CURRY PASTE

MAKES 1 JAR | ABOUT 15 MINS

3 dried guajillo chillies

1–2 red bird's eye chillies, to
   taste, deseeded and chopped

4 shallots

4 lemongrass stalks,
   roughly chopped

3 garlic cloves, peeled

A 6cm piece of fresh root ginger,
   peeled and roughly chopped

1 tbsp ground coriander

1 tbsp medium-hot
   curry powder

3 tbsp groundnut oil

*Note: The curry paste is made in
a batch that will be sufficient for
several meals, but it keeps well
in the freezer for up to 1 month.*

Remove the stem and seeds from the guajillo chillies,
then put them in a small bowl and cover with hot water.
Leave to soak for 15 minutes or until soft.

Drain the soaked chillies and put them in a food
processor. Add the bird's eye chillies and the remaining
paste ingredients. Add 3 tbsp water, then process to
a smooth paste, adding a drop more water if needed.
Spoon into a sterilised jar and keep in the fridge for up
to 1 week, or freeze for up to 1 month.

*R*amen with a kick! If you're not a fan of spice, you can leave out the chilli. This reminds me a bit of one of my favourite recipes from my last book, the tofu noodle soup, as it is so comforting and crammed full of punchy flavours.

Spicy Coconut RAMEN

SERVES 2 | UNDER 30 MINS

4 tbsp chilli and lemongrass
  curry paste (see opposite)

200g ramen noodles
50g asparagus, woody ends
  snapped off, spears cut
  into 5cm lengths
1 tbsp groundnut oil
400ml tin coconut milk
450ml vegetable stock
3 tbsp soy sauce or vegan
  fish sauce, or to taste
2 pak choi
A handful of mangetouts,
  sliced
Juice of 1 lime
2 handfuls of beansprouts
A few sprigs of fresh mint and
  coriander, to garnish

Cook the ramen noodles in a pan of boiling water for 2–4 minutes or according to the packet instructions. Drain in a colander and plunge into ice cold water, then leave to one side.

Put the asparagus spears in a pan of boiling water and cook for 2 minutes to blanch them, then drain in a colander and refresh under cold water.

Put 4 tbsp of the chilli and lemongrass paste in a wok or saucepan and add the groundnut oil. Cook over a medium heat for 4–5 minutes until fragrant and slightly intensified in colour.

Add the coconut milk, stock and soy sauce to the wok, and gradually bring to the boil. Cook for 5–6 minutes to reduce this liquid a little, which will intensify and thicken the coconut base.

Cut the leaves from the stems of the pak choi. Shred both the leaves and stems, keeping them separate. Add the stems, asparagus and mangetouts to the base and cook for 2 minutes. Add the lime juice and the sliced pak choi leaves.

Divide the noodles and beansprouts between two bowls, ladle over the coconut broth and garnish with the fresh herbs to serve.

I love an excuse to come up with more breakfast ideas — breakfast has always been my favourite meal of the day. Not every vegan wants to have a smoothie or avo toast for breakfast; we want to get creative and we want to eat flavour-packed meals. I would say this is my go-to for a Sunday brunch, or a fix for if I've been out the night before. Brussels sprouts and potatoes are two of my favourite vegetables, so by combining them we've created magic. If you don't like egg replacer, you can always scramble some tofu with it instead.

HASH with Coconut Bacon, Scrambled Vegan Egg & Harissa Ketchup

SERVES 2 | UNDER 30 MINS

220g new potatoes (or leftover
   cooked new potatoes)
2 tomatoes, cut in half
3 tbsp olive oil, plus extra
   for drizzling
½ red onion, finely sliced
1 tsp fennel seed
½ red chilli, deseeded
   and finely sliced
100g Brussels sprouts,
   finely sliced
3 tbsp vegan egg replacer
60g ketchup
1 tsp rose harissa paste
½ quantity of coconut bacon
   (see page 29)
Sea salt and freshly ground
   black pepper
2 slices of toast, to serve

*Note: This recipe is good
to make with leftover new
potatoes, if you have them.*

Cook the new potatoes in a saucepan of boiling water for 10–12 minutes until just tender. Drain in a colander. Leave until cool enough to handle, then cut into cubes.

Preheat the grill. Season the cut sides of the tomatoes with salt and pepper. Drizzle with a little oil and cook under a hot grill for 6–8 minutes until the tomatoes are starting to collapse.

Put 2 tbsp of the oil in a non-stick frying pan over a medium heat, then add the onion, fennel seed and chilli, and cook until soft. Add the potatoes and Brussels sprouts, and cook until the potatoes gain some colour. Season with salt and pepper.

While the hash is browning make the scrambled 'eggs'. Mix the egg replacer with 160ml water. Heat a small saucepan with 1 tbsp oil over a medium heat. Add the egg replacer mixture and scramble it, using a wooden spoon, for 6–8 minutes until cooked through.

In a small bowl, mix the ketchup with the harissa. Serve the hash sprinkled with the coconut bacon alongside the scrambled egg, grilled tomatoes, harissa ketchup and a slice of toast.

In my last book I had a buckwheat and banana pancake recipe, which I know many of you loved, so I had to include more pancakes in this book. These will blow your mind; they are SO similar to non-vegan crêpes! I missed having crêpes when I went vegan — the whole egg thing baffled me a bit. But a flax egg is a perfect replacement, plus flaxseed is packed with omegas and really good for you.

Flaxseed CRÊPES

SERVES 2–3 | ABOUT 40 MINS

1 tbsp ground flaxseed
140g plain flour
A pinch of salt
250ml soya milk
1 tbsp vegan margarine,
  melted, plus extra for
  greasing
Lemon juice and
  maple syrup, to serve

Put the flaxseed in a small bowl and add 3 tbsp hot water. Stir well, and then leave to gel for 5 minutes.

Sift the flour and salt into a bowl and add the milk, the flaxseed mixture and the melted margarine. Whisk together to make a smooth batter. Rest the batter for 30 minutes.

Heat a knob of margarine in a non-stick frying pan over a medium heat and add a ladleful of the batter, then swirl the pan to coat the base with the batter. Cook the crêpe until golden, then toss it or turn it over using a spatula and cook the second side in the same way. Keep the cooked crêpes warm while you repeat with the remaining batter. Serve with a squeeze of lemon and a drizzle of maple syrup. (The batter will keep in the fridge for up to 3 days but may need a splash of milk to loosen the mixture as the flaxseed will continue to swell.)

Easy to make and simply delicious, another brunch go-to — add a salad to turn this into a satisfying main meal.

SWEETCORN FRITTERS *with*
Roasted Tomatoes & Avocado

SERVES 2 | UNDER 30 MINS

220g vine tomatoes

2 tsp balsamic vinegar

Olive oil

80g plain flour

1 tsp baking powder

2 tbsp vegan egg replacer

120ml soya milk

200g sweetcorn, thawed
   if frozen

Small bunch parsley or
   coriander, leaves roughly
   chopped (optional)

Zest of 1 lime

2 spring onions, finely sliced

1 avocado, pitted, peeled
   and sliced

Pinch of chilli flakes

Sea salt and freshly ground
   black pepper

Preheat the oven to 180°C (160°C fan, gas 4). Put the tomatoes on a small baking tray and drizzle with the balsamic vinegar and 2 tsp olive oil. Season and cook in the oven for 8–10 minutes or until the skins have burst a little.

Meanwhile, sift the flour, ½ tsp salt and the baking powder into a mixing bowl and whisk together. Put the egg replacer in a bowl, add 5 tbsp ice-cold water and whisk together. Stir in the milk and pour into the flour mixture, whisking until smooth. Stir in the sweetcorn, coriander (if using), lime zest and spring onions.

Heat a little oil in a non-stick frying pan and pour in tablespoonfuls of the batter. Cook for 1–2 minutes on each side, until golden. Repeat with the remaining batter to make 6 fritters. Serve the fritters with the avocado and roasted tomatoes. Garnish with a sprinkle of chilli flakes and a squeeze of lime.

The perfect side dish to your roast: potatoes and broccoli mixed with tons of flavour. Healthy and yummy, quick and easy; this has everything you need for the basis of a quick meal or a simple dish when you're under the stress of entertaining.

Broccoli TRAY BAKE

SERVES 4 | UNDER 1 HR

600g new potatoes, whole or
   any large ones cut in half
1 red onion, cut into wedges
1 red chilli, deseeded and
   thinly sliced
3 garlic cloves, thinly sliced
½ lemon, thinly sliced
2 tsp za'atar spice mix
3 tbsp olive oil
1 head of broccoli, broken
   into florets
Sea salt and freshly ground
   black pepper

Note: This goes very well with vegan sausages or the sliced seitan on page 163.

Preheat the oven to 180°C (160°C fan, gas 4).

Cook the new potatoes in a saucepan of boiling water for 10 minutes. Drain in a colander, then cut them in half and put them in a large roasting tin.

Add the red onion, chilli, garlic and lemon. Sprinkle over half the za'atar and half the oil. Season with salt and pepper, then toss everything together to coat evenly. Roast for 20 minutes.

Rinse the broccoli under cold running water in a sieve. Put the broccoli in a bowl and add the remaining za'atar and oil, then season and toss to combine. Add the broccoli to the roasting tin and continue roasting for a further 15–20 minutes until the vegetables are tinged brown and are tender. Serve.

Layers and layers of goodness in a low-maintenance meal for when you need something tasty on the table quickly.

Harissa Roasted RED CABBAGE STEAKS

MAKES 4 | UNDER 40 MINS

1 medium-sized red cabbage,
   cut into 4 × 1½ cm slices
3 tsp rose harissa paste
4 tbsp olive oil
A handful of walnuts
Juice of ½ lemon
A small bunch of flat leaf
   parsley, leaves roughly
   chopped
A small bunch of mint,
   leaves roughly chopped
Seeds from ½ pomegranate
Sea salt and freshly ground
   black pepper

Preheat the oven to 180°C (160°C fan, gas 4) and line a baking tray with baking parchment. Put the cabbage on the prepared baking tray. Put the harissa in a small bowl and stir in the oil, then brush both sides of the cabbage slices with this mixture. Season with salt and pepper, then roast for 25–35 minutes until tinged brown and tender.

Meanwhile, put the walnuts on a baking tray and roast for 5–10 minutes until golden, shaking the pan occasionally. Finely chop the nuts.

Squeeze the lemon juice over the steaks and serve sprinkled with the herbs, pomegranate seeds and walnuts.

Crunchy on the outside, yet squidgy on the inside, these nuggets are packed with goodness. They're nothing like the chicken nuggets you may have grown up eating, and are all the better for it. This recipe takes a bit of cooking but is great for small kids and big kids alike!

LENTIL & CARROT NUGGETS
with Tamarind Date Ketchup

MAKES ABOUT 20 NUGGETS

| UNDER 2 HRS

120g red lentils, rinsed
   and drained
400g carrots, cut into
   large chunks
2 onions, unpeeled
Olive oil, to drizzle and
   for shallow-frying
Leaves from 2 thyme sprigs
4 garlic cloves, unpeeled
50g oats
Juice of ½ lemon
1 bunch coriander, leaves
   roughly chopped
1 tbsp ground cumin
½ tsp chilli powder
Sea salt and freshly ground
   black pepper

*For the tamarind and
   date ketchup:*
400g tomatoes, cut in half
4 garlic cloves, unpeeled
2 heaped tsp tamarind paste
1 tbsp date syrup
1 tbsp soft brown sugar

To coat the nuggets:
60g plain flour, seasoned
   with salt and pepper
1 tbsp vegan egg replacer
80g fresh breadcrumbs

Preheat the oven to 180°C (160°C fan, gas 4). Put the lentils in a small saucepan and cover generously with water. Bring to the boil and stir, then cover and reduce the heat. Simmer for 20 minutes, until the lentils are tender, or according to packet instructions. Drain well in a colander.

Put the carrots in a roasting tin and add the onions. Drizzle over a little oil, then sprinkle over the thyme. Cover the tin loosely with foil and roast for 25 minutes. Remove the foil from the tin and add the garlic, then return to the oven and roast for 20–25 minutes until the garlic and onions are soft and the carrots are nicely roasted and tinged brown.

Meanwhile, to make the ketchup, season the cut sides of the tomatoes with salt and pepper, then put them in another roasting tin and add the garlic. Roast for 25 minutes or until the tomatoes are starting to break down a little and collapse.

Squeeze the garlic cloves for the ketchup from their skins — they should pop out quite easily. Put the tomatoes and garlic in a sieve over a bowl and press them through the sieve with some force, using the back of a spoon, until only the seeds and skins are left in the sieve.

Put the tomato pulp and the remaining ketchup ingredients in a small saucepan over a low heat. Cook for 10–15 minutes or until it is reduced to a good ketchup consistency.

Put the oats for the nuggets into a food processor and process to a powder. Squeeze the onions and garlic from their skins and put them into the food processor with the remaining nugget ingredients. Pulse until the mixture comes together but retains texture — be careful not to over-process the mixture or it will lose its texture and become a paste. Put in the fridge to firm up for 1 hour.

Shape the nugget mixture into 20 nuggets. To coat the nuggets, dust them lightly in the seasoned flour. Put the egg replacer in a bowl, add 7 tbsp ice-cold water and whisk together. Brush each nugget with a little of the egg replacer mixture and then dip them into the breadcrumbs.

Heat a little oil in a non-stick frying pan over a medium heat and fry the nuggets until golden brown and crispy on each side. Serve with the ketchup.

Dosas are traditionally served for breakfast in India, and this dish is packed with yummy carbs — the best kind of comfort food. It does take a few days to ferment, but with a little bit of planning you'll get such a sense of achievement from making this. I love being able to make this at home as it tastes so great.

Sweet Potato
DOSA

**SERVES 4 | 2–3 DAYS FOR
THE BATTER, 1 HR TO COOK**

100g urid dhal, rinsed
  and drained
200g white basmati rice,
  rinsed and drained
2 sweet potatoes
70g red lentils, rinsed
  and drained
2 tsp coconut oil, plus
  extra for frying
4 small shallots, finely sliced
½ red chilli, deseeded and
  finely chopped
4cm piece of fresh root ginger,
  peeled and grated
1 tsp ground turmeric
1 tsp garam masala
2 tsp cumin seeds
Juice of 1 lime
A small bunch of coriander,
  roughly chopped
Sea salt and freshly ground
  black pepper
Lemon or lime wedges, to serve

Put the urid dhal and rice in a bowl and cover with water. Leave to soak for 24 hours.

Drain the urid dhal and rice and transfer to a bullet blender. Add 480ml water and blend until fairly smooth, not too grainy, and the consistency of double cream. Pour the batter into a large mixing bowl, cover and leave somewhere warm for 1–2 days to ferment. When the batter is ready it should be slightly thickened and foamy on top. Season with ½ tsp of salt.

Preheat the oven to 200°C (180°C fan, gas 6). Wrap the sweet potatoes in foil and bake for 25–30 minutes until cooked through.

Put the red lentils in a small saucepan and just cover with water. Cook for 20–25 minutes or until they are cooked through and most of the water has evaporated. You may need to top up with a little water from time to time.

Heat the coconut oil in a saucepan over a low heat and add the shallots, chilli and ginger. Cook until soft. Add the spices and continue cooking for 2 minutes or until fragrant.

Peel away the skin from the sweet potatoes and discard it, then add the flesh to the saucepan with the spices, along with the red lentils. Warm the mixture through, stirring to combine and breaking up the sweet potato a little as you go.

Heat a little coconut oil in a large non-stick frying pan (if you have a dosa or pancake pan even better) over a high heat. Add 1½ ladlefuls of the dosa batter to the pan, spreading the batter out quickly using the back of the ladle in a circular motion. Cook until small bubbles appear on the surface, flip over and cook for another 30 seconds, then turn out onto a plate and keep warm. Continue with the remaining batter to make 4 dosas.

Add the lime juice to the sweet potato mixture, add the coriander and stir through, then season with salt and pepper to taste. Divide the sweet potato mixture between the pancakes and roll up. Serve with a lime wedge on the side.

I think this recipe speaks for itself. As a lot of you may know, I am a huuuuuge pasta fan and this creamy dish is super delicious — I promise it won't disappoint.

SCHNITZEL with Noodles & Creamy Dill Sauce

SERVES 2 | UNDER 45 MINS

2 tbsp vegan egg replacer
100g fresh breadcrumbs
1 medium-sized sweet potato,
  peeled and cut into slices
  5mm thick
60g oyster mushrooms
120g tagliatelle
A knob of vegan butter
3 tbsp sunflower oil
Sea salt and freshly ground
  black pepper
Sauerkraut and cornichons,
  to serve (optional)

For the dill sauce:
150ml soya cream
Juice of ½ lemon
1 tsp Dijon mustard
A small bunch of dill,
  fronds finely chopped

Put the egg replacer in a small bowl with 120ml cold water and whisk until smooth. Put the breadcrumbs on a plate. Dip the sweet potato slices and oyster mushrooms into the egg replacer mixture, then into the breadcrumbs, coating both sides.

Cook the tagliatelle in a saucepan of boiling salted water for 5 minutes, until al dente, or according to the packet instructions. Drain in a colander and tip back into the pan, then add the butter and allow the residual heat to melt it.

While the tagliatelle is cooking, heat the oil in a large non-stick frying pan over a medium-high heat. Fry the sweet potato and oyster mushrooms in batches until golden brown and crispy all over and the sweet potato is tender inside.

To make the sauce, heat the cream in a small saucepan over a medium heat until hot. Whisk in the lemon juice, mustard and dill. Season to taste with salt and pepper.

Serve the schnitzels with the tagliatelle, drizzled with the creamy dill sauce. I also like to serve this dish with a little sauerkraut and some cornichons on the side.

This gorgeous tart is sweet and savoury at the same time; the key to perfecting it is remembering that the thinner the slices of butternut, the better. The homemade pesto takes this recipe to the next level; you can make extra and use it for other things!

Butternut Squash Tart
WITH PUMPKIN SEED PESTO

SERVES 4 | UNDER 1 HR

350g butternut squash
  (neck part), peeled and
  cut into 3mm slices
1 tsp thyme leaves
2 pinches of dried chilli flakes
1½ tbsp maple syrup
1½ tbsp olive oil
flour, for dusting
500g vegan puff pastry,
  thawed if frozen
Sea salt and freshly ground
  black pepper
Rocket, to serve

For the pumpkin seed pesto:
20g pumpkin seeds
15g pine nuts
30g basil leaves
½ garlic clove
A squeeze of lemon juice,
  or to taste
50ml extra virgin olive oil

Preheat the oven to 200°C (180°C fan, gas 6) and line a baking sheet with baking parchment. Put the butternut squash slices in a bowl and add the thyme, chilli flakes, maple syrup and oil. Season with salt and pepper, then toss together to coat.

On a lightly floured work surface, roll out the pastry to 5mm thick. Using a dinner plate or something similar as a guide, cut a circle from the pastry about 27cm in diameter. Put the pastry circle on the prepared baking sheet and, using the tip of a sharp knife, score a circle about 1cm from the edge.

Arrange the butternut slices on top of the pastry, overlapping the slices and making sure you stay clear of the scored edge. Put a sheet of baking parchment on top of the tart, and another baking sheet on top, then bake for 20 minutes. Remove the top baking sheet and baking parchment, and continue cooking for 25–30 minutes until the pastry is perfectly golden brown and puffed around the edges.

While the tart is baking, make the pumpkin seed pesto. Toast the pumpkin seeds and pine nuts in a dry frying pan over a medium-high heat for 1–2 minutes until the pumpkin seeds start to pop and both seeds are fragrant and lightly browned.

Put the seeds and the remaining pesto ingredients into a mini blender and pulse until combined. (Alternatively, you could use a mortar and pestle, adding the oil at the end.) Season with salt and pepper. Drizzle the tart with the pesto and serve with some rocket leaves.

It can be surprisingly hard to find vegan curries in UK restaurants and personally I'm not prepared to live a life without them, so I am very happy to have as many homemade recipes as possible! Easy to prepare and mild, this creamy curry is a classic for good reason.

DHAL with Roasted Cauliflower & Chapattis

SERVES 4 | UNDER 1 HR

450g cauliflower, broken
  into florets
1 tbsp olive oil
1 tsp cumin seeds
200g red lentils, rinsed
  and drained
½ tsp ground turmeric
2 tbsp coconut oil
2 banana shallots,
  finely sliced
1 onion, finely chopped
2 garlic cloves, crushed
1 tsp black mustard seeds
1 tsp ground cumin
150g tomatoes, roughly
  chopped
Sea salt and freshly ground
  black pepper

For the chapattis:
230g chapatti flour,
  plus extra for dusting
1 tsp salt
2 tbsp olive oil, plus
  extra for greasing

Preheat the oven to 180°C (160°C fan, gas 4). Put the cauliflower florets in a roasting tin and drizzle over the oil. Toss to cover in the oil, then sprinkle over the cumin seeds and season generously with salt and pepper. Roast for 25–30 minutes until tinged golden brown all over.

Put the lentils in a saucepan and add the turmeric and 800ml water. Bring to the boil, then skim off any scum from the surface. Reduce the heat and simmer gently for 20 minutes or until the lentils are cooked and a nice thick consistency.

While the lentils are cooking, heat 1 tbsp of the coconut oil a small pan over a low heat and add the shallots. Season with salt and cook until crispy and golden brown. Tip the shallots onto a sheet of kitchen paper and leave to one side.

Put the remaining 1 tbsp coconut oil into the pan and cook the onion, garlic, mustard seeds and cumin over a low heat until soft and translucent. Add the tomatoes and cook until broken down and saucy. Stir this mixture into the lentils, then season the dhal with salt and pepper.

To make the chapattis, sift the flour and salt into a mixing bowl, then make a well in the centre of the flour. Measure 150ml hot water in a measuring jug and add the olive oil, then mix together. Pour it into the well in the flour. Incorporate the water into the flour, little by little, using your fingertips.

Bring the dough together and knead for 5 minutes until soft and pliable. Divide the dough into 8 pieces and roll into small balls. Lightly oil the balls and cover with cling film, then leave to rest for 10 minutes. Liberally flour a work surface and roll each ball into a thin round disc.

Cook each chapatti over a high heat in a dry frying pan, flipping them over after they puff up to cook on both sides. Spoon the dhal into bowls, top with the roasted cauliflower and crispy shallots, and serve with the chapattis on the side.

I love pasta, all kinds of pasta, and this is an easy mid-week veggie hit. It's perfect for scaling up to make sure you have lunchtime leftovers the next day.

Mediterranean AUBERGINE PASTA

SERVES 4 | 45 MINS

2–3 tbsp olive oil

2 aubergines, cut into
   large chunks

1 red onion, finely chopped

1 tbsp dried oregano

2 garlic cloves, crushed

6 ripe plum tomatoes,
   roughly chopped

20g pine nuts

1 red pepper

300g wholemeal or plain
   penne pasta

1 tbsp red wine vinegar

A small bunch of basil, half
   the leaves roughly chopped

40g green olives, sliced

40g capers

Sea salt and freshly ground
   black pepper

Heat 2 tbsp oil in a large saucepan over a medium-high heat, then add the aubergines and season generously with salt. Cook for 5-6 minutes until the aubergines are starting to brown, lower the heat and continue cooking for 10 minutes. Add the onion, oregano, garlic and a little more oil if needed, and cook over a gentle heat for 2 minutes or until the onion is soft. Add the tomatoes to the pan and continue cooking until they break down.

Meanwhile, put the pine nuts in a dry pan and toast over a medium-high heat, tossing regularly, for 1-2 minutes, or until golden brown. Leave to one side.

Put the pepper on a baking tray and cook under a hot grill until blistered on all sides. Cover with a heatproof bowl and leave to one side until cool enough to handle. Peel off the papery skin and discard it along with the seeds. Cut the flesh into strips.

Meanwhile, cook the pasta in a saucepan of boiling salted water for 8-10 minutes until al dente, or according to the packet instructions. Drain in a colander, reserving a cup of the pasta water.

While the pasta is cooking, add the pepper to the aubergine mixture, followed by the red wine vinegar, chopped basil and olives. Heat a splash of oil in a separate pan over a high heat and fry the capers for 2 minutes until tinged brown and crispy.

Loosen the sauce a little with the pasta water if needed, then season to taste with salt and pepper. Spoon the aubergines over the penne and garnish with the whole basil leaves, the pine nuts and crispy capers.

I first made an avocado chocolate mousse when I went to a cooking class with a competition winner from my last book. When I initially saw avocado and chocolate in the same sentence I thought 'no thanks'. I was proved totally wrong, not only because this is so simple to make, but because it really tastes like divine chocolate mousse. How about that, a pudding involving one of your five a day!

AVOCADO CHOCOLATE MOUSSE
with Cherry Compote

SERVES 4 | 15 MINS

160g dark vegan chocolate,
  finely chopped, or buttons
2 ripe Hass avocados,
  halved and pitted
2 tsp vanilla bean paste
1 tbsp tahini
A pinch of salt
4 tbsp maple syrup
4 tbsp cherry compote
4 cherries with stems or
  edible flowers, to decorate
  (optional)

Melt the chocolate in a heatproof bowl over a pan of gently simmering water, making sure the base of the bowl doesn't touch the water. Stir and remove from the heat. (Alternatively, put the chocolate in a small microwave-proof bowl and microwave on full power for 30 seconds. Stir to ensure the chocolate is fully melted.)

Scoop the flesh from both avocados and put it into a food processor. Add the vanilla bean paste, tahini, salt and maple syrup, then process until smooth. While the processor is still running, trickle in the melted chocolate until combined.

Put a tablespoonful of cherry compote into the base of each of 4 stemmed glasses, and spoon in the chocolate mousse. Decorate each glass with a cherry or flowers on top, then serve.

I know what you're thinking: tofu and ice-cream? But trust me, tofu creates an amazing texture that is ideal for ice-cream and is definitely healthier than the dairy version you might be used to. It's so creamy and yummy and takes mere minutes to make.

Silken Tofu & Berry
ICE CREAM

SERVES 6 | 5 MINS PLUS FREEZING TIME

300g silken tofu

60ml agave nectar

250g probiotic coconut yogurt

2 tsp vanilla bean paste

400g frozen berry
  smoothie mix

Put the silken tofu, agave nectar, yogurt and vanilla bean paste in the bowl of a food processor and process until smooth.

Add the frozen berry smoothie mix and process again until smooth. Spoon into a freezerproof lidded container and put in the freezer until frozen to your desired consistency.

You're going to thank me for this . . . Matcha ice cream recently became one of my favourite flavours. It's not sickly sweet, but sweet enough. The colour is gorgeous, perfect if you're in the mood to try out some food styling pics (see page 198 for some tips!). If that's not your vibe, just go ahead and enjoy the flavours.

Vanilla Matcha ICE CREAM

**SERVES 3–4 | 5 MINS PLUS
FREEZING TIME**

1 vanilla pod
150g golden syrup
150ml water
240g plain soya yogurt
2 tsp matcha powder
160g soya cream
A squeeze of lemon juice

Cut the vanilla pod in half lengthways and scrape out the seeds onto a plate using a knife. Put the golden syrup and water into a small pan over a low heat and heat until combined.

In a bowl, whisk together the yogurt, vanilla seeds, matcha and cream. Pour in the golden syrup mixture and whisk together. Add the lemon to balance the acidity.

Chill in the fridge until cold, then transfer to an ice cream maker and churn according to the manufacturer's instructions. Transfer to a freezerproof container and freeze until firm enough to scoop. (Alternatively, put the mixture into a freezerproof container and freeze for 2 hours, then use a fork or an electric whisk to break up the crystals. Return to the freezer and repeat once more, then leave to freeze.) Allow to thaw for 10 minutes before serving.

Feed Me

NIBBLES

I never thought I'd be the kind of person who would run out of pitta bread and think 'ah, I'll just make some', but they're so simple — once you've realised you can make them easily there's no going back. There's nothing like warm pitta bread fresh out of the oven. If you don't have time to let these prove then you can skip that part and get them straight into the oven!

Pretty Pink PITTAS

MAKES 10 BREADS | 2½ HRS, INCLUDING PROVING

50ml olive oil, plus extra
 for greasing
7g sachet of fast-action yeast
1 tsp agave syrup
260g strong white bread flour,
 plus extra for dusting
1 tsp salt
2 tbsp powdered beetroot
1 tsp black onion seeds
 (optional)
Vegetables and hummus,
 to serve

Note: Try these with a rainbow range of fresh vegetables and the sauerkraut on page 50 or with the marinated carrot from the blini recipe on page 123.

In a bowl, mix together 170ml lukewarm water, the oil, yeast and agave syrup, then leave to one side for 5 minutes to activate the yeast. You will know it's ready when you see foamy bubbles on the surface.

Sift the flour with the salt and beetroot powder into a mixing bowl, then stir in the onion seeds, if using. Make a well in the centre and pour in the activated yeast liquid. Stir everything together with your fingertips and bring the dough together into one piece.

Tip out the dough onto a light floured work surface and knead for 10 minutes. Don't be tempted to add extra flour; the dough must be kept quite wet to allow the pockets of steam to form when in the oven. If you are struggling with the stickiness of the dough, you can use a dough scraper to help move it around.

Put the dough in a clean, lightly oiled bowl and turn it to make sure all sides are oiled, then cover with cling film and leave in a warm place to prove for 1–2 hours or until doubled in size.

Preheat the oven to 240°C (220°C fan, gas 9). Put 2 non-stick baking sheets into the oven to heat up. Divide the dough into 10 pieces and roll into balls. Leave to rest under a damp tea towel for 10 minutes. Roll each ball into a thin, even oval or round shape, then cover and leave to rest again for 10 minutes.

Working quickly, slap the pittas onto your prepared hot trays and bake for 10–12 minutes or until every pitta has puffed up. Serve warm, with the baba ganoush or the tzatziki from pages 116–117, or filled with a rainbow of veggies and hummus.

You can never have too many kinds of hummus! This beetroot one is ridiculously creamy with a hint of sweetness. Perfect for snacking on or to please guests with.

Roasted Beetroot HUMMUS

SERVES 4–5 | 30 MINS

3 medium-sized beetroot,
  cooked
2 tsp cumin seeds
1 tbsp maple syrup
2 tbsp extra virgin olive oil
400g tin chickpeas,
  rinsed and drained
Juice of 1 lemon
2 tbsp tahini
Sea salt and freshly ground
  black pepper
Toasted pitta bread, to serve

To serve:
Leaves from a small bunch
  of coriander (optional),
  chopped
1 tbsp dukkah spice mix
  (optional)
Seeds from ½ pomegranate
  (optional)
Extra virgin olive oil

Preheat the oven to 180°C (160°C fan, gas 4). Cut each beetroot into 6 pieces, then put them in a roasting tin and sprinkle with the cumin seeds, maple syrup and oil. Season well and roast for 25 minutes. Alternatively, if you're short on time, you can use vacuum-packed beetroot, without vinegar.

Put the beetroot in a food processor, add the chickpeas, lemon juice and tahini, and blitz until smooth. Add a splash of water to loosen the mixture if necessary. Season with salt and plenty of freshly ground black pepper.

Spoon into the centre of a plate or a shallow bowl. Using the back of a spoon, rock the base back and forth to spread the mixture out to form a bowl shape. To finish, sprinkle with the coriander leaves and dukkah spice, if you like. You can also add some pomegranate seeds. Drizzle over a generous glug of oil, then serve with pitta bread (see page 119) or toasted rye bread.

Making this cream cheese does require patience, but it is totally worth it. The result is truly perfect; it's hard to find store-bought vegan cream cheese that is this luxurious in flavour and texture. Once you have made it you can use it for all kinds of recipes — canapés, sandwiches, dips and even with pasta.

HOW TO MAKE *Cashew Cream Cheese*

MAKES 350–400G | 1–2 DAYS SOAKING, 12–24 HRS CHILLING, 5 MINS PREP

300g cashew nuts
½ tsp garlic powder
Juice of 2 lemons
3 tbsp nutritional yeast
1 tsp celery salt
1 tbsp chopped chives

Put the cashew nuts in a bowl and cover with water. Leave to soak for 24–48 hours.

Drain the cashew nuts and put them into a food processor with the remaining ingredients, except the chives. Add 4 tbsp water and blitz until completely smooth in texture.

Spoon the mixture into the centre of a square of muslin and draw the corners of the cloth together into the centre. Pull them up tightly around the cheese and secure them with an elastic band. Place the cheese on a plate in the fridge for 12–24 hours to firm up. Remove the cheese from the cloth, shape into a barrel shape and serve it sprinkled with the chopped chives.

*U*sing your homemade cream cheese you can create show-stopping blinis that are bound to impress. Some might think 'carrot instead of salmon, surely not?' but it will blow you away. It takes time to marinate the carrots in advance but it is KEY to getting the flavour and texture you'll want for maximum deliciousness.

BLINIS *with Marinated Carrot & Cashew Cream Cheese*

MAKES 20–25 BLINIS |
FOR THE BLINIS: 45 MINS
FOR THE CARROTS: 15 MINS
PREP, 24 HRS MACERATING

2 tbsp ground flaxseed
7g fast-action dried yeast
10g sugar
300ml soya milk or other
   vegan milk, lukewarm
80g buckwheat flour
½ tsp salt
140g strong white flour
Sunflower oil, for greasing
½ × quantity cashew cream
   cheese (see opposite)
1 tbsp chopped chives

For the marinated carrot:
200ml rice vinegar
3 tbsp caster sugar
2 tsp salt
1–2 drops of hickory liquid
   smoke (optional)
Zest of 1 lemon
3 carrots, cut into ribbons
   using a swivel peeler

To make the marinated carrot, put the rice vinegar in a bowl and add the sugar, 1 tsp salt, hickory liquid smoke (if using) and lemon zest. Stir until the sugar has dissolved.

Put the carrots in a bowl and add 1 tsp salt. Massage the salt into the carrots a little, then leave them to sweat for 30 minutes.

Transfer the carrots to a jar and leave to macerate for 24 hours.

When you're ready to make the blinis, put the flaxseed in a bowl and add 6 tbsp hot water. Stir together, then leave to one side for 2 minutes to gel. In a small bowl, mix together the yeast, sugar and milk, then leave to one side for 5 minutes to activate the yeast. You will know it's ready when you see foamy bubbles on the surface.

Sift the flours and salt together in a mixing bowl, then add the yeasty milk and the flaxseed mixture, and whisk to make a smooth batter. Cover the bowl with cling film and leave at room temperature for 30 minutes.

Heat a little oil in a non-stick frying pan over a medium heat. Cooking in batches, add tablespoonfuls of the batter to the pan. Cook until bubbles appear on the surface, then flip the blinis over using a spatula to cook the other side. Repeat with the remaining batter.

Spread a little cashew cream cheese over the blinis and top with the marinated carrot, then sprinkle with chopped chives to serve.

As a kid growing up I would order these in restaurants any chance I got, and loved to eat them piled high with cheese or sour cream. This version, using cashew cream, tastes so similar to what I used to gorge on. Great party food or for a dinner party.

CRISPY POTATO SKINS
with Salsa & Lime Cashew Cream

SERVES 4 | 2 HRS

6 baking potatoes
1 tsp garlic granules
¼ tsp smoked paprika
2½ tbsp olive oil
Sea salt and freshly ground
   black pepper

For the lime cashew cream:
100g cashew nuts
1 tsp cumin seeds
1 pinch of garlic granules
Zest and juice of 1½ limes

For the salsa:
1 small red onion,
   finely chopped
Juice of 1 lime
250g tomatoes,
   roughly chopped
2 tbsp pickled jalapeño
   chillies, kept as slices
A small bunch of coriander,
   leaves roughly chopped
1 tbsp extra virgin olive oil
A dash of Tabasco sauce,
   or to taste

Preheat the oven to 180°C (160°C fan, gas 4). Put the cashew nuts for the cashew cream in a small bowl and cover with water, then leave to one side.

Prick each potato twice with a fork, then bake for 1½ hours or until cooked through to the centre. Leave the oven on.

Mix together the salsa ingredients and season with salt and pepper.

Cut the potatoes in half and scoop out a little of the flesh — keep to use for another dish. In a small bowl, mix together the garlic granules, paprika and oil, then brush this mixture onto the inside and outside of each potato skin. Season and put on a baking tray, then cook in the oven for 30 minutes or until the skins are crispy inside and out.

Drain the cashew nuts in a colander and tip them into a blender (I think a small, powerful blender like a bullet blender works best for the proportions of this recipe) with the remaining cashew cream ingredients and 120ml water, then process until smooth. Season with salt and pepper. To serve, spoon the salsa into the crisp potato skins and top with a dollop of the cashew cream.

Arancini is an all-time favourite of mine — a little morsel of joy. You can still achieve the creaminess without dairy products, rest assured. This recipe is a tad complex; perfect if you're up for a challenge!

Pea & Sundried Tomato ARANCINI —

**SERVES 4 | ABOUT 1 HR
PLUS COOLING TIME**

400–600ml hot vegetable stock
80g peas
1 tbsp olive oil
1 tbsp vegan butter
120g shallots, finely chopped
100g leek, white part only,
  finely sliced
1 garlic clove, crushed
150g Arborio rice
250ml vegan white wine
Zest of 1 lemon, plus a
  squeeze of lemon juice
1 tbsp vegan cream cheese
50g vegan Parmesan cheese,
  finely grated
80g plain flour
100g fresh breadcrumbs
1 tbsp vegan egg replacer
100g sundried tomato paste,
  plus extra to serve
Sunflower oil, for deep-frying
Sea salt and freshly ground
  black pepper
Vegan aioli and basil leaves,
  to serve

Keep the vegetable stock simmering in a pan on the hob. Cook the peas in a small saucepan in a little boiling water for 2 minutes or until just cooked. Drain in a colander and leave to one side.

Put the olive oil and butter in a large non-stick frying pan over a low heat, add the shallots, leek and garlic, and cook until soft and translucent. Add the rice to the pan and stir it to coat with the oil, then cook for 1 minute or until translucent. Increase the heat a little and add the wine, then allow it to bubble for 2 minutes.

Add the hot stock, a ladleful at a time, allowing each ladleful to bubble away and become absorbed into the rice before adding the next, stirring continuously. Keep adding the stock until the rice is cooked but still retains a little bite — you may not need to add all 600ml of stock. This will take 20–30 minutes.

Stir in the peas, lemon zest, cream cheese and Parmesan cheese. Season with salt and pepper, and add a squeeze of lemon juice. Tip the rice onto a plate and spread it out so that it can cool quickly. When cool, transfer the rice to the fridge until completely cold.

Put the flour and breadcrumbs onto two separate plates. Put the egg replacer in a bowl, add 6 tbsp water and whisk together. Drape a small square of cling film over one hand and spoon a heaped dessertspoonful of the risotto rice into the centre, flattening it out into a flat circle with the back of a spoon. Put a small teaspoonful of the sundried tomato paste into the centre of the circle then, using the cling film to help you, wrap the edges of the rice around the filling to create a perfectly round compact ball. Repeat with the remaining risotto rice. Dust each ball in a little flour and then carefully brush with the egg replacer and roll in the breadcrumbs.

Heat the sunflower oil in a deep-fryer or large saucepan to 170°C (test by frying a small cube of bread; it should brown in 40 seconds). Deep-fry the arancini in batches until golden brown on all sides. Drain on kitchen paper.

Serve the arancini with extra sundried tomato paste or vegan aioli and a few fresh basil leaves.

We are very lucky that Jus-Rol is vegan friendly — it makes cooking anything with a pastry sooo much easier! This is a really quick and easy recipe. Pick your favourite vegan sausage brand for this one (I personally love the ones from Linda McCartney). I think these would be perfect for a kid's birthday party, but also if you just want something to snack on or take with you on the go. They taste almost identical to the original, non-vegan versions.

VEGAN *Sausage Rolls*

MAKES 20–24 ROLLS

| 45 MINS

1 × 320g sheet of ready-rolled
  vegan puff pastry,
  thawed if frozen
Flour, for dusting
2 heaped tsp English mustard
  or harissa paste (or 50/50)
6 vegan sausages
2 tbsp soya milk
1 tsp black onion seeds
1 tsp sesame seeds
Piccalilli or harissa ketchup
  (page 82), to serve

Preheat the oven to 180°C (160°C fan, gas 4) and line a baking sheet with baking parchment. Unwrap the pastry onto a lightly floured work surface and cut down the centre lengthways. Spread each rectangle with either the mustard or the harissa, or both!

Put 3 sausages running down the centre of each piece of puff pastry. Brush the edges of both pastry rectangles with the milk and fold the pastry over, pressing the edges together with the end of a spoon or your finger to seal them.

Cut the filled pastry into pieces 3cm long, and put them onto the prepared baking sheet.

Brush each sausage roll with soya milk and sprinkle with the seeds. Bake for 25–30 minutes or until golden brown all over. Serve with piccalilli or harissa ketchup.

You'll need to invest some time in this one, but you won't regret it. Jackfruit has become hugely popular and is something I've started cooking with more and more recently. If you haven't tried it before, the texture is very meaty but the actual fruit is quite plain-tasting and absorbs flavours brilliantly. For this recipe we've given it a 'pulled pork' vibe.

HOT & SPICY Pulled Jackfruit Bao

MAKES 10 BAOS

| UNDER 2½ HRS

250g plain flour, plus
   extra for dusting

¼ tsp salt

1 tsp baking powder

1 tbsp caster sugar

2 tsp fast-action dried yeast

50ml soya milk

1 tbsp sunflower oil, plus
   extra for greasing

For the pulled jackfruit filling:

1 tbsp groundnut oil

400g tin jackfruit, drained

1 tbsp gochujang

2 drops of hickory liquid
   smoke (optional)

50ml hoisin sauce

2 spring onions, cut into
   matchsticks

40g cucumber, sliced
   into rounds

Sift the flour, salt and baking powder into the bowl of a stand mixer and whisk in the sugar and yeast. Add 100ml tepid water, followed by the soya milk and oil. Fit the dough hook to the mixer and mix for 10–12 minutes until the dough is smooth and elastic. Alternatively, mix in the water by hand and bring the dough together, then transfer to a lightly floured work surface and knead for 10–12 minutes until the dough is smooth and elastic, adding in a little more flour if the dough is too wet.

Put into a clean, lightly oiled bowl, cover with cling film and leave to prove for 1 hour or until doubled in size.

Tip the dough onto a lightly floured work surface, then, using your hands, roll it into a log shape and cut it into 10 equal portions. Roll each portion of dough into a ball, then, using a rolling pin, roll each dough ball into a small oval. Lightly oil the top of each oval using your finger.

Place each oval on a small square of parchment slightly bigger than the oval itself, on a lightly oiled baking sheet. Carefully fold each oval in half over a lightly oiled chopstick — you should be able to fit two dough balls to each chopstick. Cover the bao loosely with a lightly oiled piece of cling film, then leave to prove again for 1 hour or until doubled in size.

Meanwhile, make the pulled jackfruit filling. Put 1 tbsp oil in a frying pan over a medium heat, then add the jackfruit and fry until tinged golden brown around the edges. Put the gochujang in a small bowl and stir in 200ml water, then pour this into the pan with the jackfruit. Cook the jackfruit until the sauce has reduced by about half and the jackfruit is sticky and coated with the sauce. Break the fruit down from time to time using a wooden spoon to produce a pulled texture. Add the hickory liquid smoke, if using.

Gently remove the oiled chopsticks from the bao and then use a fish slice to lay them carefully in a steamer. Steam for 10 minutes until puffed and cooked through. Prise a bao apart and spoon in a little hoisin sauce, then top with some of the pulled jackfruit, a little spring onion and a slice of cucumber. Repeat with all the remaining bao, then serve.

When you think potato salad, you think creamy deliciousness. This recipe is exactly that and more. Serve up with other salad options for the perfect spread with friends and family.

Dill & Cornichon POTATO SALAD

SERVES 2 | 20 MINS, PLUS COOLING TIME

400g new potatoes
65g vegan mayonnaise
1 tbsp lemon juice
1 tsp Dijon or English mustard
3 spring onions, finely sliced
30g cornichons,
  roughly chopped
A small bunch of dill,
  fronds roughly chopped
Sea salt and freshly ground
  black pepper

Cook the new potatoes in a saucepan of boiling water for 10–12 minutes until just tender. Drain in a colander. Leave until cool, then cut into bite-sized chunks.

Put the mayonnaise in a bowl and add the lemon juice, mustard, spring onions, cornichons and dill. Mix well, then fold in the potatoes and season to taste before serving.

These are so quick and easy to make and are extremely moreish, so beware! You won't be able to tell that these are vegan. Ideal for snacking on in front of a film or if you want something to keep friends busy while you get on with making a feast.

Cheese STRAWS

MAKES 8–10 STRAWS

| 30 MINS

100g plain flour, plus
  extra for dusting
¼ tsp baking powder
¼ tsp cayenne pepper
2 tsp English mustard powder
20g ground almonds
60g finely grated vegan
  Cheddar cheese
1 tsp poppy seeds
60g chilled vegan butter

For the pastry glaze:
30ml soya milk
1 tsp agave nectar
1 tsp mustard powder

Preheat the oven to 180°C (160°C fan, gas 4) and line a baking sheet with baking parchment. Sift the flour, baking powder, cayenne pepper and mustard powder into a mixing bowl, and add the ground almonds, grated cheese and poppy seeds. Mix together.

Rub the butter into the dry ingredients using your fingertips until the mixture resembles fine breadcrumbs. Work it into a dough, using your hands to make it come together into one piece.

Tip the dough onto a lightly floured work surface and roll out into a rectangular shape about 1cm thick. Cut into 8–10 long lengths about 1.5 cm wide and put onto the prepared baking sheet.

To make the glaze, pour the milk into a small bowl and whisk in the agave and mustard.

Brush the pastry with the glaze, then bake for 15–20 minutes or until golden brown and cooked to perfection. Cool on a wire rack.

Garlic bread is a huge weakness of mine, but it's something that I struggle to find when I'm out and about. Gone are the days when you can go out and buy one of those baguette packets to shove in the oven. For this, I am slightly grateful, for two reasons: one — I wouldn't have had this recipe come into my life and two — I would likely have to buy a whole new wardrobe. I love serving this alongside pretty much anything: stews, pasta, casseroles or with my current TV series obsession!

GARLIC *Tear-and-Share* BREAD

SERVES 6 | 2 HRS 40 MINS

400g strong white bread flour,
  plus extra for dusting
1 tsp salt
1 tsp sugar
7g active dried yeast
250ml warm soya milk,
  plus extra if needed
25ml olive oil, plus extra
  for greasing
½ lemon
100g vegan butter
20g garlic cloves, crushed
  (about 4 fat cloves)
A small bunch of flat leaf
  parsley, leaves roughly
  chopped, or wild garlic
  leaves, roughly chopped
1 tbsp polenta

For the topping:
30ml soya milk
1 tsp agave nectar
Flaked sea salt

Sift the flour and salt into a large mixing bowl, then stir in the sugar and yeast. In a small bowl, mix the milk with the oil and a squeeze of lemon. Pour the milk mixture into the flour and stir together with the end of a wooden spoon. Bring the dough together with your hands, adding a touch more milk if the dough is too dry, or a touch more flour if it is too wet. Tip onto a floured work surface and knead for 10 minutes or until the dough is soft and springy.

Put the dough in a clean, lightly oiled bowl, then cover with cling film and leave in a warm place to prove for 1 hour or until the dough has doubled in size.

Mash the butter with the garlic, a squeeze of lemon and the parsley. Grease the sides and base of a 23cm round springform cake tin with 1 tbsp of the garlic butter and dust with the polenta.

Tip out the dough onto a floured work surface and knead for 1 minute, to knock out the air. Divide the dough into 10 equal pieces and roll each piece of dough into a ball. Arrange the balls in the cake tin, putting 7 balls around the outside and 3 balls in the centre. Cover with cling film and leave in a warm place to prove for 1 hour or until doubled in size and the balls have joined together.

Preheat the oven to 220°C (200°C fan, gas 7). In a small bowl, mix the milk for the topping with the agave and use this to brush the top of the dough. Dot with half the garlic butter and sprinkle with some flaked sea salt. Bake for 25–30 minutes or until golden brown. As soon as the bread comes out of the oven, dot over the remaining garlic butter and serve straight away.

The combinations in the salad are ones that I have grown to love — the soft texture of the aubergine with the crunch of the pomegranate seeds is quite something. A fresh dish for a sunny day or if you're in the mood for something light.

Aubergine & Pomegranate SALAD

SERVES 2 | UNDER 1 HR

A pinch of saffron threads
2 large aubergines, cut into
  slices 2.5cm thick
2 tbsp olive oil
1 tsp ras el hanout
1 garlic clove, crushed
Seeds from 1 pomegranate
A small bunch of flat leaf
  parsley, leaves roughly
  chopped
Juice of 1 lemon
20g toasted pistachio nuts,
  roughly chopped
2 tbsp tahini
4 tbsp plain soya yogurt
1 tsp maple syrup
2 tbsp pomegranate molasses

Preheat the oven to 200°C (180°C fan, gas 6). Put the saffron in a small bowl and add 2 tsp hot water. Leave to one side.

Using a sharp knife, lightly score a cross-hatch over one side of each aubergine slice to allow the marinade to permeate. In a small bowl, mix the oil with the ras el hanout and garlic. Brush this mixture on both sides of the aubergine slices, then season generously with salt and pepper. Put on a baking tray and cook in the oven for 35–40 minutes until the aubergines are golden brown and have started to collapse a little.

In a small bowl, mix the pomegranate seeds with the parsley, half the lemon juice and the pistachio nuts.

Put the tahini into the bowl with the saffron water and add the yogurt, the remaining lemon juice and the maple syrup. Stir to combine well.

Stack the aubergine rounds up on a plate, sprinkle over the pomegranate and pistachio mixture, and drizzle with the saffron yogurt. Top with a drizzle of pomegranate molasses to serve.

Although this may look a bit more on the complicated side, it really isn't! Another showstopper to impress your friends, plus it's VERY aesthetically pleasing. Healthy and delicious, it's the perfect sharing option to fix any sweet tooth cravings. NOTE: Some vegans prefer not to eat figs as they involve wasps dying to pollinate them. This is very much down to personal choice, and as this is a natural process I'm happy to continue to eat figs. However, I completely understand why others wouldn't so would suggest loading up on more of the berries if that's your preference.

Fig & Berry GRANOLA PIZZA

SERVES 4 | ABOUT 40 MINS PLUS COOLING TIME

2 tbsp coconut oil
2 tbsp almond butter
60ml brown rice syrup
40g ground flaxseed
80g toasted buckwheat groats
120g oats

For the topping:
200g plain coconut or
 soya yogurt
A handful of berries
3 figs, thinly sliced
1 tbsp pomegranate seeds

Preheat the oven to 170°C (150°C fan, gas 3), and line the base of a 23cm springform cake tin with baking parchment. In a small pan, mix together the coconut oil, almond butter and brown rice syrup, then gently heat the mixture over a medium-low heat until warm and combined, stirring frequently.

Put the flaxseed in a mixing bowl and add the buckwheat and oats. Stir the syrup mixture into the oat mixture until evenly combined. Tip the oat mixture into the prepared tin and flatten it into an even layer using the back of a metal spoon. Bake for 25–30 minutes or until tinged golden brown around the edge.

Leave the granola base to cool completely in the tin on a wire rack. Once cool, remove the base to a plate or board. Spoon on the yogurt and spread it evenly over the granola base, then scatter the berries over the top. Add the fig slices and then sprinkle over the pomegranate seeds to finish. Serve.

Aquafaba is the liquid you usually throw away when draining your can of chickpeas. This magical liquid allows you to veganise a lot of egg-white-based recipes. So save up your bean water and whip up a tasty treat! This is one of those recipes you could really trick people into thinking isn't vegan — the meringues are so fluffy and crunchy, they quite literally melt in your mouth.

Eton MESS

SERVES 6 | 2–3 HRS

140ml aquafaba (bean water)
160g caster sugar
1 tsp cream of tartar
½ tsp vanilla extract
150g strawberries, hulled and
  cut in half
500ml coconut yogurt
50g pistachio nuts, crushed

For the compote:
300g rhubarb, cut into
  2cm pieces
2–3 tbsp sugar

Note: Aquafaba freezes really well, so when draining your chickpeas, why not freeze the liquid into ice cube trays and save it for a later date. Then simply defrost the aquafaba cubes in your fridge a day before you need to use them.

Preheat the oven to 110°C (100°C fan, gas ¼) and line a large baking sheet with baking parchment. Put the aquafaba in a clean grease-free bowl or the bowl of a stand mixer and add the sugar, cream of tartar and vanilla extract. Using a handheld electric whisk or with the whisk attachment for your stand mixer, whip the aquafaba mixture for 5–10 minutes or until it forms stiff, glossy peaks.

Use a small amount of the meringue mix to stick the corners of the greaseproof paper to the baking sheet. Spoon the meringue mixture into 6 equal blobs on the prepared baking sheet, spacing them well apart.

Bake in the centre of the oven for 2–2½ hours or until each meringue is completely crisp. Turn off the oven and allow the meringue to cool completely inside the oven.

While the meringue is cooking, make the rhubarb compote. Put the rhubarb in a small saucepan and add 2 tbsp sugar and 2 tbsp water. Cook over a medium-high heat for 5–8 minutes until the rhubarb breaks down and is very soft. Add 1 tbsp water if the mixture starts to dry out. If the rhubarb tastes too tart, add another 1 tbsp sugar. Set aside and allow to cool.

When ready to serve, break the cold meringues into rough pieces. Using individual glass dishes or tumblers, add layers of meringue pieces, strawberries, rhubarb compote and yogurt. Sprinkle over the crushed pistachio nuts, then serve immediately.

An all-time favourite dessert of mine! My step-mum used to make these for my sister and me all the time — they'd be waiting for us when we got back from school. The amazing thing about this recipe is that I doubt anyone would be able to guess what the caramel is made from. You will need a blender or food processor for this one, but by now I'm guessing you've made the very worthwhile investment.

Millionaire's SHORTBREAD

MAKES 25 SHORTBREADS
| 1½ HRS PLUS COOLING TIME

180g plain flour
¼ tsp salt
100g coconut oil,
  at room temperature
50g sugar
A little coarse sea salt,
  to sprinkle (optional)

For the caramel:
300g pitted dates
100g coconut oil, melted
150g coconut cream
2 tbsp vanilla extract
1 tsp salt

For the glaze:
100g vegan dark chocolate
  (60–70% cocoa solids),
  roughly chopped
2 tsp coconut oil

Preheat the oven to 190°C (170°C fan, gas 5). Sift the flour and salt into a bowl. Add the coconut oil to the flour, and rub the oil into the flour using your fingertips until the mixture resembles fine breadcrumbs. Sprinkle over the sugar and stir in 4–6 tbsp water, just enough to bring the mixture together to form a dough. If the dough feels a little dry, add a further 1–2 tbsp water.

Put the dough into a 20cm square tin. Using your hands, press the mixture into the base until you have an even layer.

Bake in the centre of the oven for 40–45 minutes until the shortbread has turned a light golden colour. Allow to cool in the tin on a wire rack for 10 minutes, then carefully remove the shortbread onto the wire rack and leave to cool completely.

To make the caramel, put the dates into a high-speed blender or food processor and add the coconut oil, coconut cream, vanilla and salt. Process at high speed until you have a smooth, glossy mixture.

Line the base and sides of your 20cm square tin with a layer of cling film — this will help you to get the shortbread out later. Put the cooled shortbread in the bottom of the tin and then pour the date caramel over the top. Use a spatula to smooth the caramel as flat as possible. Put the tin into the freezer for 30 minutes.

To make the glaze, melt the chocolate and coconut oil in a heatproof bowl over a pan of gently simmering water, making sure the base of the bowl doesn't touch the water. (Alternatively, put the ingredients in a small microwave-proof bowl and microwave on full power for 30 seconds.) Stir with a small whisk or spoon until the chocolate and oil have combined completely.

Remove the caramel shortbread from the freezer and, using the cling film as a lever, remove the shortbread from the tin and put it onto the wire rack. Put a large plate underneath the rack to catch any drips. Pour the chocolate over the caramel shortbread and, working quickly, use a spatula to spread a thin layer over the top. Sprinkle a little coarse sea salt over the top, if you like. Once the chocolate has gone from shiny to dull, it is ready to cut. Transfer to a chopping board and cut into 25 pieces. Store in an airtight container in the fridge for up to 2 weeks.

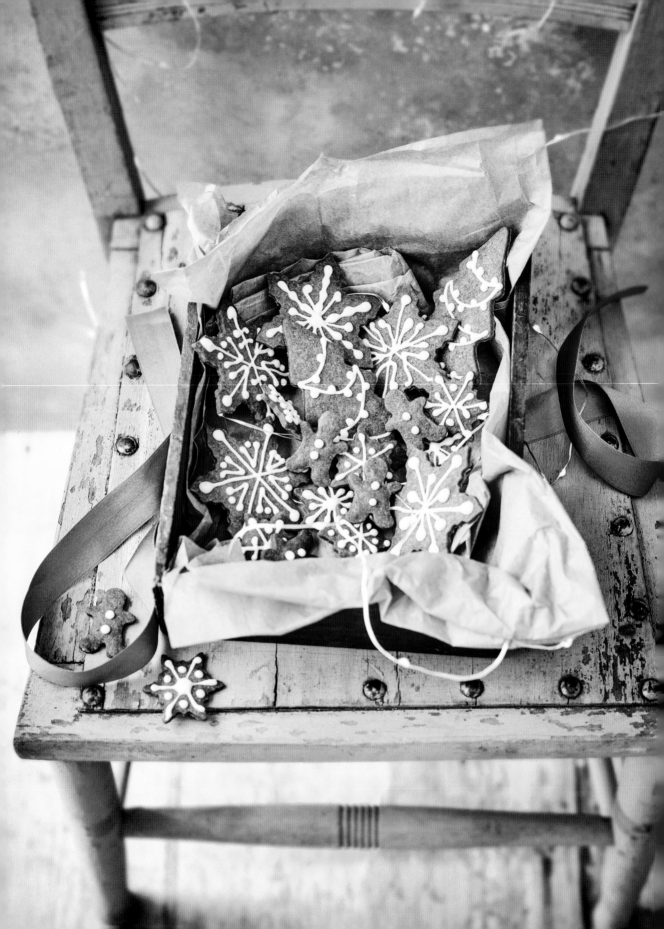

Christmas is a time for indulging, whether you're vegan or not. It's also when you spend quality time with your friends and family, so it's when I enjoy cooking and baking the most. This recipe is great if you have younger members of the family who get involved with the decorating.

Christmas GINGERBREAD COOKIES

MAKES 24–30 COOKIES

| 1 HR PLUS COOLING TIME

265g plain flour

1 tbsp ground ginger

½ tsp ground cinnamon

¼ tsp fine salt

170g soft dark brown sugar

1 tbsp black treacle

3 tbsp golden syrup

130g vegan block margarine, melted

50g vegan white chocolate (optional)

Sift the flour, spices and salt into a large mixing bowl. Add the sugar, then, using your hands, mix in the treacle, golden syrup and margarine until combined and a dough is formed. Knead the dough lightly on a work surface to incorporate any dry patches. Form the dough into a rough ball shape and cut evenly in half.

Lay a piece of cling film, about the size of an A4 sheet of paper, onto your work surface. Place one half of the dough on top and lay another A4-sized piece of cling film on top. Roll the dough evenly between the cling film sheets to approximately 3mm thick. Repeat the process for the other half of dough, then put the sheets of gingerbread dough into the fridge for 20–30 minutes to rest and firm up.

Preheat the oven to 180°C (160°C fan, gas 4) and line a large baking sheet with baking parchment. Take the chilled sheets of gingerbread dough out of the fridge. Use festive cutters to cut out your Christmassy cookies. Put onto the prepared baking sheet, spaced apart, and bake on the centre shelf of the oven for 10–15 minutes until the cookies have deepened in colour. Leave to cool completely on the baking sheet on a wire rack. Don't worry if the cookies are a little soft to the touch when they first come out of the oven — they will harden as they cool.

If you want to decorate the biscuits, melt the chocolate in a heatproof bowl over a pan of gently simmering water, making sure the base of the bowl doesn't touch the water. Spoon the chocolate into a piping bag with a snipped end or fitted with a fine piping tube. Pipe designs onto the biscuits and leave to set before serving.

Feed Me CELEBRATIONS

The perfect winter comfort food, this dish is super filling so don't overdo it! I love to have it with a side of veggies.

BUTTERNUT SQUASH GNOCCHI *with*
Sage & Toasted Hazelnuts

SERVES 4 | UNDER 2 HRS PLUS COOLING TIME

2 small butternut squash, unpeeled, cut in half lengthways and deseeded

2 garlic cloves, crushed

Leaves of 2 thyme sprigs

2 tbsp olive oil, plus extra for frying

50g potato flour

50g '00' flour, plus extra for dusting

A handful of toasted hazelnuts, roughly chopped

Leaves from a small bunch of sage

Sea salt and freshly ground black pepper

Vegan Parmesan cheese, grated, to serve (optional)

Preheat the oven to 180°C (160°C fan, gas 4). Using a sharp knife, score a cross-hatch over the flesh side of each squash half. Put on a baking tray and rub the flesh with the crushed garlic, then scatter over the thyme and season generously with salt and pepper. Drizzle with the oil.

Bake for 45–50 minutes until the squash is completely tender and tinged brown.

Scoop the flesh from the squash, discarding the skin. Put the butternut flesh in a pan over a medium heat and break it down with a wooden spoon. Continue cooking for 30 minutes, stirring regularly to remove as much moisture as possible. Leave to go completely cold.

Stir both flours into the squash purée and season with a little more salt and pepper.

Flour the work surface and roll the dough out into 3 long sausages, about 2cm wide, then cut into roughly 3cm lengths.

Cook the gnocchi in a pan of boiling salted water for 3 minutes or until they rise to the surface. Drain in a colander and leave and allow to steam-dry for a couple of minutes.

Add about 2 tbsp olive oil to a frying pan over a medium heat. When the oil is hot, add the gnocchi, hazelnuts and sage, and pan-fry until they are tinged brown on both sides and the sage is crispy. Spoon into bowls and grate over a little cheese to serve.

*W*hat better to eat when you get in from a night out or you've woken up feeling slightly the worse for wear. Maybe you're having a night in and you want something naughty to feast on? The making of this recipe is the incredible gravy, so make sure you don't leave that out! You can thank me later.

POUTINE *with*
Perfect Fries &
Mushroom Gravy

SERVES 4

Perfect fries (page 162)
70g vegan Cheddar cheese,
  grated
2 tbsp chopped parsley

Rich mushroom gravy:
MAKES 1 JUG | 1½ HRS

60g dried wild mushrooms
1 tbsp sunflower oil
2 onions, thinly sliced
2 celery sticks, finely chopped
2 tsp fresh thyme leaves
1 carrot, diced
2 tbsp tomato purée
200ml vegan red wine
2 star anise

1 bay leaf
1 tbsp Marmite or Vegemite
2 tsp vegan Worcestershire
  sauce
1 tbsp brown miso
1 tsp cornflour (optional)
2 tbsp soya cream (optional)
Sea salt and freshly ground
  black pepper

To make the gravy, put the mushrooms in a bowl and cover with 300ml hot water. Leave to one side.

Put the oil in a large saucepan over a low heat and gently cook the onions, celery, thyme and carrot for 15–20 minutes until soft and starting to colour. Stir in the tomato purée and cook for 1 minute.

Increase the heat a little and add the wine, star anise and bay leaf. Allow it to bubble away for 5 minutes.

Stir in the Marmite or Vegemite, Worcestershire sauce, miso and 800ml water. Strain the mushrooms in a sieve over a bowl and then add the liquid and the mushrooms to the pan, leaving any grit behind in the sieve. Allow this to bubble away over a medium–low heat for 1 hour or until the liquid is reduced by about half, which will intensify the flavours dramatically. You may need to top the pan up from time to time with a little water if the liquid level drops too much.

Strain the reduced liquid through a fine mesh sieve, pressing down firmly to remove all the liquid from the contents. Discard the mushrooms.

Now you can tweak the taste of the gravy: you can season with a little salt and pepper or add a little more Worcestershire sauce.

If you like your gravy thicker, mix the cornflour in a bowl with 2 tsp water, then pour it into the gravy and stir over a gentle heat until thickened. For a more indulgent creamy gravy, you can add the cream — this is my favourite!

Preheat the grill. Put the fries on a large heatproof platter and cover with the cheese, then put them under the hot grill for 1–2 minutes to melt the cheese a little. Pour over the mushroom gravy and sprinkle with chopped parsley to serve.

I used to eat gratin alllll the time — it's my weakness for anything cheesy or creamy that just gets me. This gratin recipe will not disappoint; the sauce is undeniably creamy and though I'm the kind of person who tends to add broccoli to everything anyway, the flavours here are divine. The ideal accompaniment for any family meal or if you're having people round for a roast!

Tenderstem & Cavolo Nero Gratin
WITH CIABATTA & HAZELNUT TOPPING

SERVES 4 | UNDER 1 HR

100g macadamia nuts

400ml tin coconut milk

2 tbsp lemon juice

1 tbsp vegan
Worcestershire sauce

1 tsp mustard powder

½ tsp freshly grated nutmeg

2 tbsp nutritional yeast

1 tbsp olive oil, plus
extra for drizzling

1 onion, finely chopped

2 garlic cloves, crushed

1 bay leaf

220g Tenderstem broccoli

100g cavolo nero,
woody stems removed,
roughly chopped

80g ciabatta bread,
torn into large chunks

A handful of chopped
hazelnuts

Zest of 1 lemon

Preheat the oven to 180°C (160°C fan, gas 4). Put the nuts in a small bowl and pour over hot water to cover. Leave to soak for 10 minutes. Drain in a colander.

Put the soaked nuts in a food processor or blender and add the coconut milk, lemon juice, Worcestershire sauce, mustard powder, nutmeg and nutritional yeast, then process until perfectly smooth.

Heat the oil in a saucepan over a medium heat and add the onion and garlic. Cook for 5 minutes or until soft and translucent. Pour in the coconut milk mixture and add the bay leaf. Very slowly, using the lowest heat setting, bring the mixture to the boil, to allow the bay leaf to infuse the coconut milk. Remove from the heat.

Blanch the Tenderstem broccoli in hot water for 3–4 minutes until just tender. Add the cavolo nero to the water for 30 seconds right at the end of the cooking time. Drain, then put the Tenderstem and cavolo nero into a suitable baking dish. Pour the coconut mixture over the top of the green vegetables, then top with the ciabatta, hazelnuts and lemon zest. Drizzle with a little oil and bake for 20–25 minutes or until bubbling and the ciabatta is golden brown and crispy.

If you're in the mood for a feast for your friends then this is definitely a great contender! When you think vegan pie you might not necessarily get too excited but I can promise you that this one will exceed expectations. Even without dairy products, this is deliciously creamy, and the mushroom texture beautifully complements the kale.

Creamy Mushroom & Cavolo Nero PIE

SERVES 4 | 1 HR

2 tbsp olive oil, plus
  extra if needed
550g chestnut
  mushrooms, sliced
300g mixed wild
  mushrooms, sliced
1 tbsp tamari
4 garlic cloves, crushed
1 red onion, finely chopped
150g cavolo nero or kale,
  woody stems removed,
  roughly chopped
2 tsp brown miso
225ml soya cream
½ lemon
500g vegan puff pastry
  or shortcrust pastry
Flour, for dusting
30ml soya milk
1 tsp agave syrup
Sea salt and freshly ground
  black pepper
Creamy mashed potato and
  green beans, to serve

Preheat the oven to 220°C (200°C fan, gas 7). Put the oil in a large non-stick saucepan over a medium heat and add the mushrooms and a good pinch of salt. Cook for 15–20 minutes until tender, stirring until all the water has been released and evaporated. Add the tamari and stir to coat the mushrooms and give them a rich dark-brown colour. Remove from the pan and leave to one side.

Add the garlic and onion to the pan, with a splash more oil if needed, and cook until soft and translucent. Remove from the pan and add to the mushrooms.

Add the cavolo nero to the pan and increase the heat, then add 125ml water and cook until the leaves have wilted and all the water has evaporated. Return the mushroom mixture to the pan.

Put the miso in a bowl and stir in 100ml hot water, then add this to the pan followed by the cream and a squeeze of lemon juice. Season to taste with salt and pepper, adding a squeeze more lemon juice if needed.

Spoon the filling into a 28cm pie dish. Roll out the pastry on a lightly floured work surface until roughly the thickness of a pound coin and a bit larger than the pie dish and its rim. Brush the edge of the pie dish with a little water. Trim a strip of pastry 1cm wide from the outside edge of the rolled pastry and stick it around the edge of the pie dish — this will help to secure the lid. Cut a circle from the remaining pastry about 1.5cm bigger than the pie dish to make your lid.

Cover the filling with the pastry lid, pressing down firmly to secure. Trim off the excess pastry using a knife, and pierce two holes in the centre of the pie to allow the steam to escape.

Put the milk in a small bowl and whisk in the agave syrup. Brush this glaze over the pastry. Bake for 25 minutes or until the pastry is golden brown and cooked to perfection.

Quiche? QUICHE?! When was the last time you had one of those? Well this one is totally egg- and dairy-free and I'm pretty sure you won't even realise. I love to make one as it's great for sharing . . . Or just keep it in the fridge and have a slice or two for lunch here and there. It's super filling and can be eaten hot or cold.

ASPARAGUS & DILL QUICHE *with* Caramelised Shallots

SERVES 4–6 | 1 HOUR 15 MINS

2 tbsp vegan butter

200g shallots, finely sliced

2 tsp agave nectar

320g ready-rolled
  shortcrust pastry

125g asparagus,
  woody ends snapped off

Olive oil, for brushing

320g medium-firm tofu,
  roughly chopped

100ml soya cream

2 tsp Dijon mustard

3 tbsp nutritional yeast

40g finely grated vegan
  Parmesan cheese

Zest of 1 lemon and
  a generous squeeze
  of lemon juice

2 tbsp chopped fresh dill

Sea salt and freshly ground
  black pepper

Dressed salad, to serve

Preheat the oven to 180°C (160°C fan, gas 4). Melt the butter in a non-stick frying pan over a medium heat and cook the shallots with the agave for 10–15 minutes or until soft and caramelised. Leave to one side.

Line a 20cm loose-based flan tin with the pastry sheet, pressing it down into the base and up the side. Roll the rolling pin over the top to cut off the excess pastry. Prick the bottom of the pastry all over with a fork. Put a sheet of baking parchment on top of the pastry and fill with dried beans, then put in the oven to bake blind for 15 minutes. Remove the baking parchment and beans, and bake for a further 5 minutes. Leave the oven on.

Brush the asparagus lightly with oil and season generously with salt and pepper. Heat a griddle pan until searing hot and griddle the asparagus for 2 minutes or until char marked from the pan but still al dente.

Put the tofu into a food processor or blender and add the cream, mustard, nutritional yeast, Parmesan cheese, lemon zest and juice. Process until perfectly smooth and silky. Stir in the dill and season to taste.

Spoon the shallots into the base of the quiche and spread out into an even layer, then top with half the tofu mixture followed by half the asparagus. Pour in the remaining tofu mixture and finish by arranging the remaining asparagus on top. Bake for 20–25 minutes or until set. Leave to cool a little before slicing. Serve with a dressed salad.

Or what I like to call a melt-in-the-middle chocolate pudding. *licks lips* I used to buy these ALL the time and have them as an after-school or dinner treat. The spongy cake mixed with the gooey centre is just the perfect combination and has my mouth watering just thinking about it! Every second making this one is worth it — just make sure you allow time.

Chocolate FONDANT

SERVES 4 | 45 MINS
PLUS 2–3 HRS FOR FREEZING
THE GANACHE

40ml sunflower oil, plus
   extra for greasing
30g cocoa powder, plus
   extra for dusting
110g plain flour
½ tsp bicarbonate of soda
½ tsp salt
90g soft dark brown sugar
100ml soya milk
1 tsp instant coffee
1 tsp red wine vinegar
2 tsp ground flaxseed

For the frozen ganache:
100g dark chocolate
   (60–70% cocoa solids),
   roughly chopped
100ml soya milk

Note: For an extra twist, you can add a teaspoonful of peanut butter in the centre of each fondant with the frozen ganache.

Make the frozen ganache the evening before, if possible; however, if you are short of time, 2 hours in the freezer should do the trick.

To make the ganache, melt the chocolate with the milk in a heatproof bowl over a pan of gently simmering water, making sure the base of the bowl doesn't touch the water. Stir occasionally with a small whisk or spoon until the chocolate has melted and is combined with the milk. (Alternatively, put the ingredients in a microwave-safe bowl and microwave at full power for 30 seconds. If there are still lumps of chocolate, put it back into the microwave in 10-second blasts, stirring each time, until completely combined and smooth.) Pour the ganache into an ice cube tray and put into the freezer. Leave to freeze for at least 2 hours.

Thirty minutes before you want to serve your fondants, preheat the oven to 180°C (160°C fan, gas 4). Take 4 small individual pudding moulds or ramekins that will comfortably hold an ice cube, grease them with oil and dust with a layer of cocoa powder.

Sift the flour, cocoa powder, bicarbonate of soda and salt in a large mixing bowl. Using a whisk, mix the sugar into the dry ingredients.

In a separate bowl mix together the milk, 150ml warm water, the coffee, vinegar, flaxseed and oil. Using the whisk, mix the wet ingredients into the dry ingredients until the batter is combined.

Fill each pudding mould to about a quarter with the fondant mixture, then place a frozen cube of ganache on top. Cover the ganache with more fondant mixture until the pudding mould is just over half full. Gently tap the moulds on the work surface to remove any air bubbles.

Put the filled moulds onto a baking tray and bake in the centre of the oven for 14 minutes — do not be tempted to open the oven door!

When the timer goes, remove from the oven immediately. Gently release the sides of each pudding using a small round-bladed knife. Put a small serving plate on top of the mould and flip upside down so that the plate is now the right way up. Carefully lift off the pudding mould. Serve immediately with an extra dusting of cocoa powder.

Growing up, this was one of my favourite puddings, and when my mum used to make it we would 'help out' with the making — I have fond memories of licking the bowl with all the cream (the best part was the cream, obviously). This tastes so similar to the dessert of my childhood memories, and it's a fun one to make.

Tiramisu

**SERVES 6–8 | 1½ HRS
PLUS COOLING TIME**

240g plain flour
1 tsp bicarbonate of soda
1 tsp salt
195g caster sugar
150ml soya milk
1 tbsp lemon juice
80ml vegetable oil
1 tsp vanilla extract
Cocoa powder, for dusting
50g dark chocolate
   (optional), grated

*For the nut and
   chocolate ganache:*
250g cashew nuts
200g dairy-free white
   chocolate, roughly chopped
80ml plus 190ml soya milk
½ tsp of salt
1 tsp vanilla extract
1 tsp nutritional yeast

For the coffee mix:
4 cold double espresso
   shots or 300ml very
   strong cold coffee
2 tbsp dark spiced rum,
   or to taste
1 tbsp sugar

Preheat the oven to 190°C (170°C fan, gas 5), and grease and line a 20cm square cake tin with baking parchment. Sift the flour, bicarbonate of soda and salt into large mixing bowl, then whisk in the sugar.

Create a well in the centre of the dry ingredients and add the milk, 150ml water, the lemon juice, oil and vanilla extract. Using the whisk, slowly incorporate the ingredients until the batter is smooth. Pour into the prepared tin and tap the tin on the work surface to remove any air bubbles.

Bake in the centre of the oven for 40 minutes or until a skewer inserted into the centre comes out clean. If there is still raw batter on the skewer, bake for a further 5–10 minutes. Allow to cool in the tin on a wire rack for 10 minutes, then carefully remove the cake onto the rack and leave to cool completely.

While the cake is cooling, start the ganache. Put the cashew nuts in a bowl and pour over boiling water to cover. Leave to soften for 20 minutes.

Using a serrated knife, level of the top of the cooled cake and then slice it horizontally in two. Cut each half into 8 equal finger-shaped pieces.

Put the white chocolate, 80ml milk, salt and vanilla extract into a heatproof bowl over a pan of gently simmering water, making sure the base of the bowl doesn't touch the water. Allow to melt, stirring occasionally until well incorporated. (Alternatively, put the ingredients in a microwave-proof bowl and microwave on full power for 1 minute. Stir until the chocolate mixture is completely combined and smooth. This will take a moment, so be patient and allow the heat of the bowl to do the work for you.)

Drain the nuts and put them into the bowl of a high-speed blender or food processor. Add the ganache, the 190ml soya milk and the nutritional yeast, and blend until completely smooth.

For the coffee mix, put the ingredients into a bowl and stir to combine. Add an extra 1–2 tbsp rum if you like it on the boozy side.

Now for the fun bit: assembly! Take a serving dish and create the base layer by dipping each sponge finger, one at a time, into the coffee mixture. Use the first 8 pieces to line the base of the dish.

Pour half the ganache mixture on top of the soaked sponge fingers and level off with a spoon or spatula. Dust with a generous layer of cocoa powder. Repeat the process for the second layer and finish with another dusting of cocoa powder. For an extra chocolatey hit, scatter the grated dark chocolate over the top. Chill in the fridge for 1 hour or until firm, then serve.

*B*y the time you've finished making this, you won't want to eat it because it looks so pretty! This is such a great option for a birthday party or special celebration because it really is stunning. Taste-wise, what can I say? Better than any non-vegan chocolate tart I've ever had, mainly because it doesn't make you feel all sicky if you have that extra slice. Win-win really.

Raspberry & Chocolate TART —

SERVES 8–10 | 1 HR PLUS AT LEAST 2 HRS TO SET

120g sunflower seeds

15g pumpkin seeds

40g desiccated coconut

65g cacao nibs

175g pitted dates

A pinch of fine salt

45ml coconut oil, melted

100g good-quality seeded
  raspberry jam

75g raspberries

Fresh or freeze-dried
  raspberries and pumpkin
  seeds, to decorate

For the ganache filling:

300g dark chocolate
  (60–70% cocoa solids),
  roughly chopped

300ml tin full-fat
  coconut milk

A pinch of salt

Preheat the oven to 200°C (180°C fan, gas 6). Put the sunflower seeds, pumpkin seeds and desiccated coconut on a baking try and toast in the oven for 10 minutes or until the coconut has turned golden brown.

Put the hot seeds and coconut into a food processor or blender and add the cocoa nibs, dates, salt and coconut oil. Blend on high speed until the mixture comes together. Scrape down the sides of the bowl and blend again if necessary.

Tip the mixture into a 23cm tart tin. Using your hands, press the mixture around the tin until it evenly covers the base and side. Put the tart tin in the fridge to firm up slightly while you make the filling.

To make the ganache, melt the chocolate with the milk and salt in a heatproof bowl over a pan of gently simmering water, making sure the base of the bowl doesn't touch the water. Stir occasionally with a small whisk or spoon until the chocolate has melted and is combined with the milk. (Alternatively, put the ingredients in a microwave-safe bowl and microwave at full power for 30 seconds. If there are still lumps of chocolate, put it back into the microwave for 10-second blasts, stirring each time, until completely combined and smooth.)

Take the tart base out of the fridge and coat the inside with a layer of raspberry jam. Use the back of a spoon to help you smooth the jam onto the base. Tear the raspberries into pieces and sprinkle them on top of the jam layer. Pour the ganache into the tart case to fill almost to the top, leaving a little room for movement when you transfer the tart to the fridge. Chill the tart in the fridge for at least 2 hours to set the ganache.

To decorate, top with raspberries and sprinkle over some pumpkin seeds for extra crunch.

Christmas is the ultimate feasting time of year and why shouldn't you have an almighty Christmas cake to show off to everyone?! Not to mention blow them away with fantastic tastes — moist and spongy cake packed with familiar Christmassy flavours. I know sometimes these family occasions can be awkward, especially when not everyone in the family is vegan or supportive, so that's why the best thing to do is turn up with cake!

Christmas CAKE

MAKES 1 × 20CM CAKE

| 2–3 HRS PLUS OVERNIGHT SOAKING

165g currants
220g raisins
165g sultanas
55g halved glacé cherries
55g candied citrus peel
55ml brandy, plus 50ml
 brandy for feeding the cake,
 plus extra if needed
Zest and juice of 1 orange
Zest and juice of 1 lemon
385g wholemeal flour
½ tsp salt
1 tsp bicarbonate of soda
½ tsp mixed spice
½ tsp ground cinnamon
¼ tsp ground allspice
190g vegan block margarine,
 at room temperature,
 cut into 1cm pieces
2 tbsp ground flaxseed
190g soft dark brown sugar
2 tbsp black treacle
130ml soya milk

For the decoration:
100g apricot jam
2 tbsp lemon juice
A selection of dried
 fruit and nuts

The day before you intend to make the cake, put the dried fruit, glacé cherries and candied peel in a large bowl. Add the 55ml brandy and the orange and lemon zest and juice. Cover with cling film and set aside for 24 hours.

Preheat the oven to 170°C (150°C fan, gas 3). Grease and line a 20cm cake tin with a double layer of baking parchment, leaving an extra 5cm of paper above the edge of the tin to fold over later.

Sift the flour, salt, bicarbonate of soda and spices into a large mixing bowl. Rub the fat into the flour using your fingertips until it resembles fine breadcrumbs. Make the equivalent of 2 eggs by putting 2 tbsp ground flaxseed in a small bowl and mixing in 6 tbsp warm water. Add this to the flour mixture, followed by the remaining ingredients, except the brandy for feeding, then stir until there are no dry spots and everything is combined.

Tip the mixture into the prepared tin and level the top with a spatula. Bake in the centre of the oven for 2 hours or until a skewer inserted into the centre comes out clean. If the skewer has any raw cake mixture on it, return the cake to the oven for an extra 5–10 minutes and test again.

Allow the cake to cool in the tin on a wire rack for 10 minutes, then carefully remove the cake from the tin and leave it on the rack to cool completely, still wrapped in the paper.

Use a skewer to prick several holes in the top of the cake. Carefully drizzle the 50ml brandy into the cake using a teaspoon, making sure each teaspoonful is absorbed before you add another.

Keep the baking parchment around the cake, folding over the extra paper at the top, then wrap in two layers of cling film and store in an airtight container. You can make this cake up to 3 months before you need it. Simply feed it with more brandy every 2 weeks to allow the flavours to develop.

When you are ready to serve, put the jam in a small pan and add the lemon juice and a splash of water. Heat over a low heat until it forms a syrup-like texture. Arrange the dried fruits and nuts on top of the cake and brush over the glaze. Leave to set.

I could eat these all year round, but they taste so much sweeter at Christmas. They're great for wrapping up and giving to people as little gifts — homemade food is such a great way of spreading the love.

Mince PIES ———

MAKES 24 MINCE PIES

| 2 HRS PLUS COOLING TIME

1 large or 2 medium Bramley
  apples, unpeeled, quartered,
  cored and cut into small dice
2 tsp ground mixed spice
½ tsp ground cinnamon
¼ tsp ground cloves
¼ tsp ground ginger
½ tsp fine salt
100g vegetable suet
150g raisins
150g sultanas
100g prunes, finely chopped
100g mixed candied peel
175g soft dark brown sugar
Zest and juice of 1 orange
Zest and juice of 1 lemon
2 tbsp brandy
1 tbsp dark spiced rum

For the shortcrust pastry:
400g plain flour
½ tsp salt
200g vegan block margarine,
  cut into 1cm pieces

For the glaze:
2 tbsp soya milk
1 tbsp agave nectar
  or maple syrup

Put the diced apples in a large heavy-based saucepan. Add the spices, salt, suet, mixed dried fruit and candied peel, sugar and citrus zest and juice. Stir well to unsure that everything is evenly distributed. Cover and cook over a low heat, stirring occasionally to stop the mixture from sticking to the base of the pan. Once the fat has melted and the apple has softened, turn off the heat — this should take about 20 minutes. Allow to cool for 10 minutes then stir in the brandy and rum. Leave to cool completely.

To make the pastry, sift the flour and salt into a large bowl and add the margarine. Rub the fat into the flour using your fingertips until the mixture resembles fine bread-crumbs. Add 4 tbsp very cold water and, using a knife, mix to form a firm dough. If there are still any floury spots at the bottom of the bowl, add another 1 tbsp water.

Wrap the dough tightly in cling film and leave to rest in the fridge for 30 minutes.

Preheat the oven to 220°C (200°C fan, gas 7) and lightly grease two 12-cup mince-pie trays. Roll out two-thirds of the pastry to about 3mm and, using a 7cm cookie cutter, cut out as many discs as you can. Then re-roll the scraps into a ball and repeat until you have 24 discs.

Repeat the process for the remaining one-third of pastry, this time using a 6cm cutter. Line each cup of the mince-pie trays with the larger discs, then fill each one with 1–2 heaped teaspoonfuls of filling.

Brush some water around the top of each mince pie, then press and seal the smaller rounds onto the top to form a lid. Using a fork, pierce the top of each lid. To make a glaze, mix the milk with the maple syrup and use to brush over the top of each pie.

Bake for 20–25 minutes until the pastry has turned golden brown. Release the pies from the tray while still warm and transfer them to a wire rack to cool completely.

Weekly MEAL PLAN 2

A week of recipes for when you feel
like a bit of a health kick

Monday

Breakfast
Beetroot, Ginger
& Hibiscus Tea
SMOOTHIE

Lunch
TEMPEH SALAD

Snack
Super-Green
JUICE

Dinner
Chipotle Black
Bean & Quinoa
Soup WITH CORN

Tuesday

Breakfast
Beetroot, Ginger
& Hibiscus Tea
SMOOTHIE

Lunch
Chipotle Black
Bean & Quinoa
Soup WITH CORN

Snack
Super-Green
JUICE

Dinner
Mediterranean
RICE BOWL

Wednesday

Breakfast
Matcha SMOOTHIE

Lunch
Healthy NOODLE
JAR

Snack
Chocolate &
Ginger ENERGY
BALLS

Dinner
Super-Green
SOUP

Thursday

Breakfast
CASHEW BIRCHER
with Roasted
Rhubarb

Lunch
Super-Green
SOUP

Snack
Edamame Dip
& Black Rice
PROTEIN POT

Dinner
MOROCCAN
COUSCOUS BOWL

Friday

Breakfast
CASHEW BIRCHER
with Roasted
Rhubarb

Lunch
MOROCCAN
COUSCOUS BOWL

Snack
Chocolate &
Ginger ENERGY
BALLS

Dinner
Stuffed PEPPERS

Saturday

Breakfast
SWEETCORN
FRITTERS

Lunch
POMELO SALAD
with Sesame-
Crusted Tofu

Snack
Edamame Dip
& Black Rice
PROTEIN POT

Dinner
Spicy Coconut
RAMEN

Sunday

Breakfast
Acai BOWL

Lunch
Warming Vegetable
& White Bean
Stew

Snack
Ginger, Carrot &
Orange JUICE

Dinner
Chilled Cucumber,
Mint & Almond
SOUP

VEGAN *Beauty*

Sometimes you get home of an evening and really need some pampering . . . and putting together a vegan facemask is the perfect solution. In order to make sure that I was bringing you the best possible suggestions for your skin I spoke to BYBI Beauty, who make 100% natural, vegan and cruelty-free beauty products. Great huh?! Their recipe below is perfect for putting together to give yourself a bit of 'you time'.

If you're a fan, do check out BYBI Beauty and their sister company, Clean Beauty Co, for more products, recipes and tips!

www.bybi.com   @bybibeauty
www.cleanbeautyco.com   @cleanbeautyco

GREEN GODDESS FACEMASK

All of the goodness of these superfoods can benefit your skin as well as being good for your inside. Rich in omega and essential fatty acids, avocado hydrates and replenishes skin. It also helps to protect and repair damaged skin and boost collagen production. Combining it with potassium-rich banana makes for a rich and creamy texture that'll truly moisturise and brighten. The star ingredients here though are really the spirulina and matcha. Just as you would add them as a boost to your smoothie or coffee, these powerful powders add a kick to an already great facemask. Matcha is a wonderful antioxidant that helps to protect and repair damaged skin while spirulina is high in vitamin E that will nourish.

½ ripe avocado
¼ ripe banana
1 teaspoon spirulina
1 teaspoon matcha

Mash together the avocado and banana to form a smooth paste. Add the spirulina and matcha and stir until evenly distributed. Apply to face and neck, and leave for 15 minutes before rinsing thoroughly with warm water.

FOOD *Styling*

No cookbook happens on its own, and I'm so lucky to have an incredible team behind me who work to make sure that every recipe not only tastes amazing, but also looks amazing. Food styling is a carefully honed skill, but in order to help your food shots look Insta-ready, Kate Wesson, who styled the food in the book, offers some tips below.

Any photographer knows that lighting is key, and this is as true of your food as it is your face! For a perfect food shot, position your dish — if you can — next to a good source of natural light. Turn out any overhead electric lights and get close to the window. A north-facing light is best, or experiment with an overhead natural light source. This will help to bring out the colour and texture of your food and your dishware, without too much glare.

Think about your setting in terms of the story you want your shot to tell. Try to avoid anything too stagey — the props you include should make sense in real life. And don't forget about backgrounds — you don't want a shot full of kitchen cabinets or the dishwasher! But you can often create a really elegant impression by using some simple background textures, whether it's propping up a piece of card for a face-on shot, or using a gorgeous piece of textured cloth or even craft paper as a table 'cloth' for an overhead shot.

Look for eye-catching textures — overlaying different textures can add interest to an image. Don't feel that everything has to be picture-perfect glossy. Props with a bit of character can really make an image stand out. Things you might ordinarily throw away — weathered chopping boards, frayed cloth, distressed wooden surfaces, faded porcelain and chipped enamel — often look fabulous in food photography.

The colours you choose say a lot, both in terms of the context you want to create and the visual impact of the food which, after all, is the real star of the show. Don't be afraid to get creative with contrasting colours — a dish that includes a bright burst of pink pickled radish or pomegranate seeds will look fabulous on a jade green background. Layering colours can also add a great sense of depth — try stacking different blues or greys to create a sophisticated contemporary feel.

Most importantly, the food has to look good! One great tip for making sure the food looks fresh and appealing is to add chopped herbs, freshly ground pepper or other garnishes. That way even a casserole that's been in the oven for hours looks freshly prepared. But try, again, to keep it natural — a garnish is rarely placed in perfect symmetry on a dish in real life, and in an image this can look overly staged. A bit of mess looks more natural and appealing. Try chopping your herbs with scissors to get some interesting outside edges with more shape, or scatter a few crumbs on the edge of your plate.

INDEX

A BIG *thank you to . . .*

Going into this process for a second time around I really didn't think my expectations could be exceeded, but how wrong I was. From start to finish the whole team were a dream to work with and each was as fun and exciting as the last.

I want to thank the development team at Whitefox for their organisation and putting everything together so well, in particular Annabel Wright who assisted every day and made sure everything ran smoothly.

Thank you to Kate Wesson for her incredible recipe development and for opening my eyes to so many new things! Her food styling is beautiful and her relaxed energy made the whole process so much more fluid.

A special thanks to my 'bestie' Mike English, we always have a laugh working together and your hard work and attention to detail never disappoints – the photos are beautiful.

To Amy Kinnear for her resourceful prop styling and even helping out with the cooking on some of the days.

Summer and Lamphane, my hair and make-up team, you guys are always by my side and I loved mixing it up a bit on this project! Thank you also to Zoe for dressing me in some cute and colourful outfits that tied everything together so nicely.

I am grateful to my brilliant team at United Agents: Ariella, Matt and Harry, for pushing me to pitch for a second book – best decision ever! Thank you for everything you do.

Once again, the whole team at Little, Brown have been a dream to work with - Rhiannon, Hannah, Stephanie, Beth, Aimee, Tracey, Bekki and Nithya. You are a huge part of what makes this whole process so enjoyable and I honestly don't think I could ask for a better team to work with.

Last but not least, I want to thank my family and friends for their constant support, especially my mum, Tiffany and James who all made an appearance in the book and are my constant test dummies when I cook!

SPHERE

First published in Great Britain in 2018 by Sphere

Recipe Development and Food Styling: Kate Wesson
Photography: Mike English
Props Styling: Amy Kinnear
Book Design: Anna Green at siulendesign.com
Make-up: Summer Dyason
Clothes Styling: Hannah Beck
Hair: Lamphane at Michael Van Clarke
Select props from Mutts and Hounds, Rose and Grey, Naked Dye, The Invite Shop, Kana London,
   Bryony Kinnear, Jane Theophilus
Project management by whitefox
Pumpkin turmeric porridge recipe © Veganvore Limited 2018

1 3 5 7 9 10 8 6 4 2

A CIP catalogue record for this book is available from the British Library.

ISBN 978-0-7515-7340-4

Printed in Germany.
Papers used by Sphere are from well-managed forests and other responsible sources.

Sphere
An imprint of
Little, Brown Book Group
Carmelite House
50 Victoria Embankment
London EC4Y 0DZ

An Hachette UK Company
www.hachette.co.uk

www.littlebrown.co.uk